Philosophical Relativity

Peter Unger

UNIVERSITY OF MINNESOTA PRESS

Minneapolis

Copyright © 1984 by Peter Unger.
All rights reserved.
Published by the University of Minnesota Press,
2037 University Avenue Southeast, Minneapolis, MN 55414
Printed in the United States of America.

Library of Congress Cataloging in Publication Data

Unger, Peter K.
  Philosophical relativity.
  Includes bibliographical references and index.
  1. Relativity. I. Title.
BD221.U535 1984   120   83-6593
ISBN 0-8166-1233-1
ISBN 0-8166-1235-8 (pbk.)

The University of Minnesota
is an equal-opportunity
educator and employer.

Philosophical Relativity

For Susan

Contents

viii / Contents

Preface

The present essay attempts to examine two related hypotheses: the hypothesis of semantic relativity and, somewhat more important, the hypothesis of philosophical relativity. The latter hypothesis is meant to apply to philosophical problems of knowledge, certainty, power, freedom, causation, and explanation and, by implication, to still other broad topics or areas. As one might expect from the author, these hypotheses are at least fairly radical. But it is my hope that, by the book's end, the impartial reader will see the conjectures to be less radical, and to be more plausible, than they first appear.

Roughly, the book is divided in two. The first three chapters present positive arguments for the hypotheses and for their application to traditional problem areas; the last three chapters focus on answering what are, to my mind, the main objections to the positive efforts. But this division is very rough. Certain objections are brought up and answered near the beginning, and, in my opinion, some rather positive points are made in the last chapter of the book.

I am well aware that the positive argumentation is very far from conclusive. I am also aware that what will be considered serious objections by some are hastily treated by me or, as sometimes happens, are not even brought up for cursory treatment. To a certain extent, such selectiveness is inevitable in any philosophical work that seeks to address a number of broad issues. If the present essay is especially selective, as it might be, that will be understandable enough. For, even though I hope to say some things both true and important, I seek more to stimulate fresh thinking than to win converts to my approach.

Much of this essay was stimulated and sharpened by conversation and correspondence with David Lewis. My debt to him is very large indeed.

ix

A lot of the book was sharpened and clarified by discussion with John Richardson, to whom I am very much indebted.

The book's last chapter in large measure grew out of discussion with Thomas Nagel, who influenced other parts of the book as well.

Many other people offered helpful criticisms and suggestions. Although I cannot mention them all, let me give special thanks to Allen Hazen, Daniel Polowetsky, David Rosenthal, and William Wilcox.

Much of the material in chapter V appeared in my paper, "The Causal Theory of Reference," published in the journal *Philosophical Studies*. I thank the journal's editor, John Pollock, and publisher, D. Reidel, for their kind permission to use that material here.

For his work in preparing the index, my thanks go to James Sapienza.

Philosophical Relativity

I

The Hypothesis of
Philosophical Relativity

It is generally believed that the traditional problems of philosophy have definite objective answers: It is not a matter of arbitrary convention what answer one is to give to these problems. This is a more widely held, more basic philosophical belief than any belief, more specific, as to where the right answers lie. In a limited way, I mean to question this widely held conviction: I do not intend to refute the belief, which may well be impossible anyhow; nor do I expect even to offer arguments against it so compelling that many will abandon the conviction. My aim really is more modest: to cast doubt, perhaps a considerable amount of doubt, upon this generally unquestioned view about philosophical problems.

1. Problems without Solutions

The belief to be questioned is an extremely pervasive one. It is at work both with those traditional problems on which there is a great majority of philosophers on one side and also with those on which philosophers are more or less evenly divided. In each case, the belief that there is an objectively right answer is shared by those who dispute what that answer is.

An example of a problem with a fairly even division of advocates is the problem of determinism's consequences: If determinism is true, and everything that *happens* is the *inevitable outcome* of prior considerations, then what of presumed free action, of our ability to do otherwise, of moral responsibility? Many *compatibilists* all hold that we will still act freely and so on, while many *incompatibilists* hold the opposite. What both large groups have in common is the belief that there is a definite answer to the problem disputed; they disagree only on the more specific question as to what that objective answer is.

3

4 / The Hypothesis of Philosophical Relativity

A problem on which a great majority stands on one side is the problem of knowledge. Almost all philosophers hold that we know quite a lot about the world, nearly all that we claim to know. The few skeptics about knowledge hold that we really do not know anywhere near that much, extreme skeptics in the matter holding that we know nothing at all to be the case. But, along with their unceasing dispute, the majority and the skeptics alike believe in an objectively right answer. It is just that, with regard to the question of whether or not we know, the former hold that (the right answer is that) we do while the latter hold that (it is that) we do not.

The belief in objectively right answers pertains to all, or to almost all, of the traditional philosophical problems. But the debates on these problems, as to where the answers lie, appear endless. And little solid progress toward a solution as satisfactory as it is definite ever seems made. Even in the case of problems on which there is (almost) always a great majority on a certain side, as in the problem of knowledge, we have this unfortunate situation. Indeed, majority philosophers are rarely long satisfied with any given justification, or set of considerations, for the positive answer favored. Each generation of positive advocates is, of course, disturbed by the force of opposing skeptical considerations. But, in addition, and unfortunately for the idea of solid progress, each group is largely dissatisfied with the attempts to meet this force offered by the preceding generations.

Why do these debates go on and on with so little in the way of results? In all likelihood, there is no single answer to this higher-level question that will serve well for all, or even for almost all, of the traditional philosophical problems. Rather, perhaps a number of different answers will divide the territory, with some overlap. Indeed, certain problems may require several partial explanations, each account appropriate to just one of the unyielding aspects of the problem in question.

In the case of some problems, the explanation of the lack of solid progress may be cruelly simple: The problems are just too hard for the likes of us, with our certainly finite, and even rather limited, intellectual capacities. In other cases, there may be no important lack in our abilities, but the state of our "general knowledge to date" may not be developed enough to point to the objective answer. Perhaps much later on, with many further scientific and other developments, we will be in a position to see the answer to these problems or at least to settle objectively one of their key aspects. Perhaps the traditional problem of mind and body, or one of its aspects, falls in this category.[1]

The explanations of failure so far suggested are perfectly compatible with the general belief in objective answers to philosophical problems. But we should also consider an answer to our higher-level question that is not compatible: For certain traditional problems, perhaps there really is no objective answer, neither positive nor negative, neither "commonsensical" nor "skeptical." I suspect that this might explain, at least in large measure, the unfortunate situation with the two problems on which I have been focusing, as well as with a number of other philosophical problems.

2. Philosophical Relativity and Semantic Relativity

On this suggestion, the answer one prefers for a certain philosophical problem will depend upon what assumptions one has adopted in relation to that problem. And, irrespective of the problem in question, assumptions crucial to one's answer will always be somewhat arbitrary, not determined by objective facts, including facts of logic and language. A certain set of assumptions yields one answer, another set another; whatever facts pertain to the problem fail to decide between the one set and the other.

Where such a situation exists, if it ever really does, we may say that there is *philosophical relativity*. One position on a philosophical problem is to be preferred only *relative to* assumptions involved in arriving at its answer to the problem; an opposed position is to be preferred only relative to alternative assumptions; there is nothing to determine the choice between the diverse assumptions and, hence, between the opposed positions.

How might there arise such a situation of philosophical relativity? One way it might arise is through considerations of language, through semantic considerations. A crucial aspect of a philosophical problem may depend on the meaning of, or on the semantic conditions of, certain linguistic expressions in terms of which the problem is directly and standardly formulated. For example, the problem of knowledge might thus turn upon the meaning of 'know' as it occurs in typical sentences of the form 'Someone knows that such and such is the case'. In much the same way, which answer one gives to the problem may turn on one's specification of the truth-conditions of such sentences. Even if there are other aspects of a given philosophical problem that are not undecidable, the existence of only one undecidable semantic aspect may be enough to lead to philosophical relativity in the case of that problem.

Suppose that there is no objectively right answer as to how a certain expression should be interpreted; no unique determinate meaning to be assigned. In such cases, if there really are any, we will have *semantic relativity*: One set of assumptions leads to one semantic interpretation, another set leads to another, and there is nothing to decide objectively in favor of either set. If this is the case with 'know', then there is no objectively right answer as to what 'know' means. And, if that is so, then there may be no objectively right answer to the problem of whether or not we *know* such and such to be so.

To develop the idea of philosophical relativity, we may look to developing the idea of semantic relativity. To make the latter thought plausible, we should suppose it to apply fairly generally to expressions of our language, and to those of related natural languages, and not only to terms that are of direct philosophical interest. Semantic relativity, thus developed generally, might then have specific application to various philosophically conspicuous expressions: 'know', 'certain', 'cause', 'explain', 'can', 'free', and others. From these applications, our strategy runs, there may arise cases of philosophical relativity.

3. Contextualism and Invariantism

In discussions of language, few things may be taken as even relatively basic: On the one hand, there are certain people (or other "users") making marks or sounds. On the other hand, there are certain effects achieved on people as regards their conscious thought, their experiences, and, most important, their behavior. Everything linguistic, in between, is an explanatory posit.

Where such posits are made, observable phenomena—and even all objective (concrete) facts—get left behind. Then, we might expect a certain latitude, or room for descriptive maneuver, where alternative formulations may have equal claims to propriety. This suggests the idea that, for a given group of speakers, there is no single semantics that is the unique, objectively real semantics of that group. Rather, we may formulate various explanations of the people's production of effects on each other, each formulation assigning a different semantics for the population. Different total explanations of behavior each allow for a different semantic approach.

We may argue for semantic relativity in terms of an apparent conflict between two semantic approaches: *contextualism* and *invariantism*. As we shall develop them, each of these views is only vaguely conceived. For example, we leave open the question of whether a person who is a contextualist with regard to a certain range of expressions will treat some other range in an analogous manner. Even with this vagueness, however, there are enough cases of apparently different treatment for the two approaches to serve as two "reference frames" for semantics. Our argument will be that these two frames are relativistically related.

For our argument to get going, we want a bit of background: Suppose that, in a normal context and manner, someone utters the words, or the sounds that we take to express the words, 'That field is flat'. Then, in the presence of a certain field and a certain audience, this speaker thus may get that audience to "focus upon" some such thought, idea, or proposition as this: that, according to the standards for surface shape most relevant in the audience's then current context, that field is flat. Now, intuitively, there is a certain "absolute character" to words like 'flat' and 'straight', which feature may be vaguely appreciated by a helpful visualization. Without being terribly contentious, I trust, we may build on this intuition so that we may specify the proposition the audience is gotten to focus on like this: that, *according to those contextually relevant standards, that field is sufficiently close* to being such that *nothing could ever be flatter* than it is. Perhaps using the adverb 'absolutely' somewhat as a term of art or of abbreviation, we may then conveniently refer to the proposition just specified in this way: that, according to those contextual standards, the field is sufficiently close to being *absolutely* flat.

The adaptation of induced behavior is as flexible as it is subtle. For example, a speaker may be aware or may strongly believe that his hearers want to play croquet and are discussing the surface shapes of various fields with such an end in view. Even so, he may say different things to different groups of hearers all sharing that end. He may do this even if, as we may further suppose, any decent croquet game requires a field that is, so to say, at least fairly flat as far as flatness for fields goes.

Suppose our speaker believes, correctly, that a certain group he is addressing consists of croquet duffers, or novices. Then, he may well say about a certain candidate field, "That field is flat." The duffers will, in normal circumstances, then think that the field indicated is sufficiently (close to being absolutely) flat for their sporting interests. They will, we may presume, proceed to use that field and have an enjoyable game.

Later on, suppose as well, our speaker addresses a different group; he correctly believes them to be croquet masters. About the field previously discussed, he may well say to them words to the opposite effect, "That field is not flat." Ordinarily, they will avoid that field that, we may suppose, had irregularities sufficient to interfere significantly with the high standard of play, precision stroking, that they require of themselves for sporting enjoyment. For *they* will think the indicated field *not* sufficiently (close to being absolutely) flat for *their* sporting needs. When things go well, the speaker will indicate to them some *other* field, less irregular and bumpy, and say about it the prompting words, "That field is flat." Then, they, too, will proceed to enjoy themselves. Each group of players behaves toward the environment in a way suitable for the satisfaction of its members.

On still another occasion, our speaker may address the masters differently, recognizing them to be mildly inebriated and wanting more in the way of jolly sporting fun than an enjoyably excellent game. They might want a field somewhat more level than the minimum suitable for the duffers even so, but not all that much more. In some such circumstances, the speaker might say to the masters, regarding the first field, "That field is flat." They will, presumably, then proceed to use it and have a suitably jolly time.

Our use of language allows us to modify each other's behavior so that, typically, we all have a somewhat better time of things; our goals are attained; at least certain desires are satisfied. Adaptive behavior, we theorize, proceeds from adaptive, contextually relevant thinking and belief. (For most purposes of this essay, it will be enough to mention the adaptive thought itself and to inquire how it manages to take hold. But, of course, we take the same attitude toward the relevant psychological states and processes as we take toward language: They are correctly attributed only to the extent that they serve to explain, however directly or obliquely, purposive behavior, actual and potential. So, implications for behavior, and its adaptation to context, will never be at any great remove.)

In understanding linguistic behavior, we employ a distinction, often appropriate and useful, between what, on the one hand, the agent actually said to be so and, on the other hand, what he merely suggested, informally implied, or whatever. Since it appears to have some very clear cases, this useful distinction seems about as well off, overall, as most that we employ. For example, one utters the words "He is closer to fifty years of age than to forty." Now, what one stated, or actually said to be so, is *perfectly consistent* with the proposition that his age is eighty-seven; for it is true of an eighty-seven-year-old man that his age *is* closer to fifty than to forty, indeed, by a good ten years. What one suggested or only implied, however, is that the man's age is *between* forty and fifty, which is *not* consistent with the statement that the man is eighty-seven. Since what one said to be so *is* consistent with this proposition of great age, while what one suggested is *not*, the two are clearly different in this case. As with almost all of our distinctions, however, there are various cases in which this present one does not admit of such clear-cut application. Let us see what possibilities for linguistic explanation might arise from the vagueness in this distinction.

Consider, again, the little conversation between our speaker and, say, the croquet duffers. As agreed before, the speaker did, in one way or another, get his audience to attend to, to have a belief in the truth of, a thought or proposition that *related to the context* of the conversation. Uncontentiously enough, we agreed, this was the proposition that, *according to contextually relevant standards*, a certain indicated field is *sufficiently close* to being such that *nothing could ever be flatter*, is *sufficiently close* to that logically absolute limit. So, our speaker got everyone involved to focus on, even to believe in, such a contextually sensitive and relevant thought. And he did this, we may also agree, by saying what he said. But, then, we may still ask this: *What was it* that the speaker *said to be so*; what *statement* did he *make*; what is the thought or proposition (attended to or not) that the speaker actually *expressed*? Even with quite a lot of agreed background, such a question, I suggest, might be equally well answered in two very different ways.

A certain sort of semanticist, whom we will call a *contextualist*, will hold that our speaker stated, or said to be so, the very thing on which he got his audience to focus. Presumably, he then achieved this effect in a *most simple manner*, by just saying the very thing on which the audience was to concentrate. But, in that case, the thing said, which will include an implicit reference to a contextual standard, will *not itself be any simple thing*. And, since the sounds and words uttered will be relatively simple in form, there will then be only a rather *com-

plex relation between these items and the complex "statement" made by way of them. So, this contextualist approach may have certain disadvantages along with its advantages. Whatever its credits and debits, most contemporary philosophers usually hold to such a contextualist line. For a contextualist interpretation fits well with the idea that, in the main, our *ordinary statements* are actually *true* or objectively correct.

Another philosopher may hold that what our speaker actually stated was nothing so contextual and so complex. Rather, the proposition he really expressed was a relatively simple one, without even implicit inclusion of any sensitive standards. On this view, which we will call *invariantism,* what is stated is more simply related to the speaker's sounds and words: that field is (perfectly, absolutely) *flat.* To emphasize the pristine severity of the invariant content, this might perhaps be put more elaborately as: that field is such that nothing could ever be flatter. There is no additional content about contextually relevant standards or sufficient closeness. This simplicity of semantics is itself all to the good. But, then, on this invariantist position, the way the speaker got his audience to light on the relevant thought will be far from simple or so would be its description in appropriately connecting terms.

If we put the matter in terms of reasoning, an appropriate description might run like this: By trading on suitable premises concerning the context, and understood by the conversational participants, the speaker gets his hearers to infer from an (obviously) irrelevant falsehood he expressed to a relevant (presumed) truth then attended. The attended proposition is just the one that the contextualist acknowledged: that, according to contextually relevant standards, that field is (sufficiently close to being absolutely) flat. On that (indirectly) achieved basis, the audience may then proceed to play croquet or to plant peanuts or perhaps to play baseball. Behavior adaptive to context is thus induced, serving salient purposes and goals.

When it involves (unconscious) pragmatic reasoning, but also even when it takes a less highly intellectual form, the associated psychology of invariantism should be worked out in more detail. There are, I suggest, no insuperable difficulties in spelling out some such plausible stories, to the extent that we ever do detail our accounts of purposive linguistic behavior. But the complexity required here, in the detailing of an appropriate psychology, is a notable disadvantage in the invariantist's total explanatory view. So, like contextualism, his approach has its debits as well as its credits. In all events, invariantism fits well with traditional skeptical positions about our ordinary statements; it will give the skeptic the demanding conditions he wants for the key terms of his negative arguments. Knowingly or not, in various skeptical writings I have been an invariantist.[2]

Both invariantists and contextualists agree on what may be taken as the basic facts of typical linguistic situations: the sounds employed by the speaker and, at the other end, the effects on behavior achieved by way of those sounds.

Disagreement appears to occur only at some intermediate point and regarding only some "higher level" of description, where an aim at explanation is taken by way of posited items and processes. For terms, sentences, and statements posited for use in these explanations, the invariantist says that the semantics will be quite simple. Then, he must admit some other factors, at a substantial remove from semantics, that are correlatively complex. In apparent opposition, the contextualist says that it is the asssociated processes that are simple while the semantics is complicated.

Which position is the correct one; which incorrect? According to the *hypothesis of semantic relativity*, it is just a matter of how one chooses to distribute the acknowledged complexities. Either chosen distribution, this hypothesis says, is relevantly arbitrary, not fully determined by any objective facts of the matter. So, neither position is the more accurate; neither is correct to the exclusion of the other.

According to this thesis, there simply is no fact of the matter as to the (full) semantics of the relevant expressions. It is not that there is some very difficult discovery to be made, as to which position is right, a finding that will always remain beyond our all too limited reach. That other situation often obtains, of course: What was the blood type of Thales? Turning to matters of language and behavior: What was the thousandth to the last (Greek) word that Thales spoke? These questions, I presume, do have genuine answers; we will never, I also presume, have those answers. The difficulties are (rather purely) epistemological ones. In the case of these two questions, epistemological problems occur to an extremely great degree. As concerns the (full) semantics of 'flat', however, the problems are not (just) epistemological, however extreme. Rather, our hypothesis directs, there simply is nothing to discover, never was nor ever will be, as to whether the contextualist is correct or whether the invariantist is. That is the import of semantic relativity.

As I am understanding them, neither contextualism nor invariantism is an utterly extreme, absolutely sweeping semantic position: The invariantist allows that many sentences, and many terms, will be evaluated semantically according to context. How else, after all, could we explain the conditions of a typical use of 'She wasn't there last week'? And the contextualist allows that many (other) expressions will be evaluated without regard to their context of use, for example, 'At times in the history of the universe, stones exist'.

The apparent differences between these two approaches will concern a range of "intermediate" ordinary expressions. In this range, which we may regard as vaguely delimited, we find the ordinary predicate 'flat' and, thus, the containing sentence 'That field is flat'. Does the semantic evaluation of this sentence involve context only for the demonstrative subject term 'that field' or for the predicate as well? The contextualist says it is both; the invariantist says it is just the former. It is in regard to such intermediate expressions, and such aspects of their evaluation, that questions of apparent disagreement arise. It is in regard to these questions that, according to the hypothesis of semantic relativity, there is no unique, determinate answer. In that it may be thus considered as appropriately modest in scope, the envisioned relativity is not easy to dismiss.

Various distinctions commonly made in the philosophy of language, and usually rightly so, might be adduced now in an effort to dismiss invariantism and, with it, semantic relativity. But I suggest that this would involve a misapplication of these linguistic conceptions. For example, we may often distinguish between what a speaker means, in or by uttering a certain sentence, and what that sentence means; we may often distinguish, that is, between the speaker's meaning and the sentence's meaning. This is helpful in disambiguating utterances, in explaining various sorts of informal suggestions, including various figures of speech, in noticing successful communication by a speaker who is mixed up about vocabulary, and so on. But it will not serve to resolve our present problems: For the invariantist, as much as for anyone, when the speaker says "That field is flat," what he means is that a contextually indicated field is sufficiently close to being absolutely flat so as to satisfy contextually relevant purposes. But what the uttered sentence means, the invariantist maintains, is that such a field is absolutely flat (no matter about any purposes). This is the gap, or the difference, we have seen so often before, described now in somewhat different words.

The contextualist, for his part, will use the locutions of the distinction to insist that the offered gap does not exist, implying that any complexities in the situation must lie elsewhere. Therefore, he will say that, in such ordinary cases as our examples illustrate, the speaker's meaning and the sentence's meaning are relevantly the same or run in parallel or are as close as one pleases. The hypothesis of semantic relativity, confronting the same general point as before, says what is expected: In such ordinary cases, there is no objective fact of the matter, whether or not the speaker's meaning and the sentence's meaning significantly diverge.

We do not have the space here, of course, to canvass each of the numerous generally useful distinctions philosophers have drawn to discuss one or another of the indefinitely many aspects of linguistic behavior. But, as far as I can discern, none of these conceptions, however subtle, and however fruitful elsewhere, does anything much to resolve those matters that are our present object of study. Rather, each of the distinctions, it appears, is all too seminally vague. So, it seems, there are just more things to say *this* way, then more *that* way, and nothing, in the nature of the case, to decide between them.

4. Alternative Psychologies

This semantic relativity cannot be denied, I believe, by an attempt to locate some objectively telling psychological processes. For our two approaches to language can be contrasted in terms of how the psychological complexity, posited to explain adaptive behavior, enters a most appropriate explanatory story.

By making semantics itself a complex matter, the contextualist presents the acknowledged psychological complexity in a certain form. Just as sentences are sensitively complex, so grasping the meaning, or the truth-conditions, of a sentence is a suitably complex psychological act or process: Hearing only such a simple utterance as "That field is flat," the audience, in an appropriately complex mental act, grasps a complex meaning as thus offered. Typically, the hearer will then understand a complex statement to be made.

For the invariantist, such acts of grasping and understanding are simpler, no more complex than acts required by the simple linguistic items and properties that invariantism posits. In his explanatory description of the relevant mental activity, the invariantist has the complexity enter the story in a different way.

The alternative form for complexity is the key idea for the invariantist's psychological account. Within this leading conception, there is a fair amount of room for alternatives of detail. Some of the options are highly intellectual, stressing patterns of unconscious reasoning. The work of H. P. Grice on suggestion and inference in conversation shows that a good deal of unconscious reasoning is wanted by any account of our purposive linguistic behavior, even a contextualist account.[3] Of course, Grice's available writings do not give anything like a fully detailed account of these inferential situations. Insofar as such an account is available, however, it can be of particular use to an invariantist philosopher. He will just say that there is *more* such Gricean inference at work than has (usually) been suggested, outlining the additional areas, or levels, that his explanations would locate. Invariantism's use of unconscious pragmatic reasoning is only more extensive than the contextualist's, a difference in *degree,* not kind. And, as we have emphasized, this difference of degree is made up for by *other* such differences in the invariantist's explanations: He has a *less* complex semantics, and *less* complex psychological acts of semantic understanding performed, than does the contextualist.

Other psychological options for invariantism are less highly intellectual, describing the associated mental matters in terms of habits formed and followed. To a considerable extent, the recognition of such adaptive habits is appealing anyway, to be desired by any ambitious philosopher. Perhaps David Hume has done most to lead the way here. In our own day, Humean ideas have been developed by David Lewis, though, of course, here too much remains to be done.[4] Along these lines, we again have a difference that is only of degree, not kind. The invariantist posits *more* such adaptive habits than does the contextualist that are at a (further) *remove from* the population's semantic understanding. Again, such differences in degree can be compensated for elsewhere, and the invariantist does appear to pay back the debt.

Which of these psychological options should the invariantist more properly choose? We need not decide this matter. Indeed, compatible with our hypothesis, there might even be a further relativity here within the larger one that we are exploring.

5. Events in Real Time and in Real Brains: Alternative Interpretations

Psychological processes occur in real time and, presumably, in real places, perhaps mainly in our heads. Might there be some real differences in time or space that, if discovered, would tend to settle matters in favor of one of our semantic approaches? In this connection, might there be some telling experiments to be performed? We cannot dogmatically rule that there can be no such possibility. But such an eventuality seems implausible.

An invariantist might state his position by saying that first a simple semantic condition is grasped and only then is there a complex psychological process that moves the mind to focus on a contextually relevant proposition. But this way of putting things can be unfortunate. For it may suggest that invariantism expects only a little brain activity upon the hearing of a relevant sentence as compared to the prediction of contextualism and more activity later on. Then, one might arrange an experiment to see how much activity occurs how early.

What outcome would favor invariantism; what would favor contextualism? I doubt that any outcome would favor either position. For one thing, there is no saying just how much early activity a contextualist should expect, presuming he expects more, or how little an invariantist must predict. More important, there is no real reason to suppose that an invariantist should expect any less early activity than a contextualist.

Let us grant that the most brain activity will occur in connection with the assessment of context and the bearing of it on the main thought attended. Why should an invariantist hold that this assessment must occur late in the game? No reason. Exactly when the semantic import of the sentence is being grasped, for an invariantist a simple enough act, a more complex assessment of context may be occurring as well. Then, the two may be related by further complex psychological activity, but perhaps simpler than all the activity put together, that was going on just before.

Indeed, an invariantist can hold, if experiment seems to warrant it, that the very first thing we do is perform a rather complex act of contextual assessment: Before grasping semantic import at all, a person first sets the stage on which his semantic act will have some point. In that way, the invariantist can explain an experimental outcome in which first there is lots of activity, then a little, and then a lot again.

The particular way of putting invariantism that suggested a telling temporal

experiment was just an unfortunate rendering. Stripped of its temporal suggestions, the formulation is harmless enough, of course, perhaps even helpful in
some contexts. But then we must be prepared to do the necessary stripping, to
have our understanding of the position be appropriately flexible.

As it goes with time, so with space. Suppose someone gets the idea that a
certain part of the brain performs semantic acts, another part performing further
associated psychological activity. Then, it might be suggested that we experiment, with appropriate presentations of our relevant sentences, to see how much
activity is performed by each part. A lot of activity in the semantic part might
favor contextualism, a little invariantism. But will such an outcome really do
much to affect such a decision?

I do not think so. As before, there is the problem of deciding how much is
too much for the invariantist; there is no antecedent standard. Of more interest,
we note that no part of us comes labeled antecedently, as semantically operative
or not.

A certain part of the brain may perform many (contextual) semantic acts
and, in addition, many acts that are only at a remove from any semantic grasping. In the event of the experimental outcome lately indicated, an invariantist
might propose an explanation along just those lines. He could say that, in
relevant regards, the *nonsemantic* (contextual) psychological activity occasioned
by the sentences *in question* was quite similar to the *semantic* (contextual)
activity required by *less controversial* sentences, for example, by 'She was there
yesterday'. In that there is an acknowledged difference in the two groups of
sentences themselves, for example, between 'It is *flat*' and 'It is *there*', this
auxiliary hypothesis would not be implausible. In all events, I cannot see any
absurdity in such a proposal or any damage that it does to an invariantist construal of linguistic behavior.

We have disarmed, I believe, the suggestion that certain experimental outcomes would favor contextualism, disconfirming invariantism. Of course, there
is the alternative suggestion that other outcomes would weight things the other
way. But the obvious variant of the above discussion casts just as much doubt on
that opposite proposal. Semantic relativity appears, then, to be a hypothesis
that is as persistent as it is pervasive.

6. Two Levels for Relativity: Words and Objects

Just as semantic relativity may apply to 'flat' at the "level of language," so
a correlative thesis of relativity may apply at the "level of objects" to *flatness*,
or the property of being flat. Do actual perceived objects or surfaces have this
property? Are any real fields, or tabletops, *flat?* That will depend on what
'flat' means. If it means what the contextualist says, then, given the (presumed)
arrangements of matter, the likely answer is yes; if the invariantist is right about

the meaning, then the answer looks to be no. But, if there is no determinate answer to this matter of meaning, no objective way to decide between the semantic proposals, then there will be no objective answer to the question about the tabletops. It will not be determinately true that many *are* flat, and it will not be objectively true that many such objects are *not* flat. This matter of their shape just will not be an objective, determinate matter at all.

Flatness is not, to be sure, something that we deem of any great or intrinsic importance. Accordingly, questions of flatness, even those that might seem conceptually most difficult, are not standard philosophical questions. In contrast, certainty, knowledge, power, and freedom are deemed more deeply important by us, and difficult problems regarding these things are paradigmatically philosophical. Because of this, 'flat' is not a term of very much interest to philosophers, one whose semantic study cries out for attention, while 'know', 'certain', 'free', and 'can' attract quite a lot of philosophical scrutiny. But the phenomenon of semantic relativity, if it exists, does not care about this distinction. Rather, it appears relevantly democratic, pertaining to many terms of much philosophical importance as well as to many of no philosophical importance.

If semantic relativity pertains to various of our philosophically conspicuous terms, then a hypothesis of philosophical relativity may apply, at the "object level," to the matters for which those terms give a standard expression. For example, if there is no determinate answer as to the semantics of 'certain', then there may be no objective answer to the questions of whether various things (or propositions) are certain or not and to the question of whether various people are certain of various things. Similarly, if the semantics of 'know' and of 'can' are not determinate, then there may be no objective answer as to whether we know quite a lot about the world or to the question of whether we can do many things that, in fact, we do not do. Such indeterminate cases, if they exist, are instances of philosophical relativity.

7. Indeterminacy of Translation and Holistic Explanation

There will be room for semantic relativity just when there are no objective facts that determine the semantics of a given expression. In such cases, if there really are any, we will have *semantic indeterminacy* for that expression. It is this indeterminacy that is resolved only relative to different psychological assumptions, assumptions that are themselves not fully determined by any objective facts.

When indeterminacy is mentioned in connection with semantics, thoughts turn to the work of W. V. Quine. In chapter 2 of *Word and Object*, Quine argues for a thesis of the *indeterminacy of translation*.[5] In the first instance, this thesis is meant to concern semantic relations between the expressions of linguistic communities that are, in relevant regards, causally unconnected; the thesis is first put forth, that is, for cases of *radical translation*.

For Quine's thesis to be of philosophical interest, it must not depend, even in the most radical case, on radical differences in the lives or environments of the linguistic communities in question. If only one community has encountered a certain species of animal and has a word for it, it is neither plausible nor interesting to think the other community will have an expression that translates. The other community will not have an equivalent word, nor can it be expected to have available a complex definition.[6] No; Quine's thesis is meant to concern even those cases, and those matters, in which our lives and environment are relevantly the same as those of some aliens. That is why his main example concerns, not some exotic jungle beast, but rabbits, things of a sort with which we are just as familiar as are the aliens whose linguistic behavior we are to interpret.

If Quine's thesis is right even for his most radical case, then there is, as Quine no doubt realizes, no place for it to stop. The thesis must apply just as well, even if less obviously, to cases in which translation is not so radical.

The specification of the semantics for some terms of a given language by means of other expressions of that same language may be viewed as the minimal, or perhaps the degenerate, case of translation. It is at the other end of a spectrum of cases from that at which translation is most radical. In providing a semantic account of 'flat' in English, for example, we are *in effect* giving a translation of the term into a more complex expression of its own language. Are we actually giving a translation? Perhaps to say we are is not an ordinary use of the common word 'translation', but any departure from custom will be of no philosophical harm. Indeed, this (extended) use of 'translation' suggests a consequence of the indeterminacy thesis. If there is the indeterminacy of translation Quine first envisages, from jungle talk into English, then there will be indeterminacy, too, in our own attempts to state, in English, the semantics of our ordinary English expressions. Quine is prepared to accept this consequence.

Because we argue that human natural languages exhibit semantic relativity and that this relativity requires some indeterminacy of translation, we can, as we must, argue for a hypothesis of indeterminacy of translation. Even if in only an extended sense of 'translation', an English-speaking contextualist gives one translation for, say, 'That field is flat', and an invariantist gives another. There is no fact of the matter as to which of these translations is correct, which incorrect. Moreover, both the contextualist and the invariantist interested in our 'flat' may be, say, Chinese. Then, in an *unextended* sense of 'translation', their two translations of the English term may be appropriately, and equally well, provided. According to our hypothesis, there is no fact of the matter as to which of these Chinese translators is the more correct.

This argument for indeterminacy of translation applies only to cases where a language contains expressions to which our hypothesis of semantic relativity applies: These are the languages that call forth plausible treatments from invariantists and contextualists. This group includes, I suggest, any language with tenses or with modal constructions, as well as any with absolute terms. And there are other sorts of problematic expressions as well. For this reason, I suspect that the indeterminacy thesis applies to all natural languages actually employed by human beings.[7]

As I understand him, Quine is convinced that his thesis will apply to any workable language whatever, even to those with only the most straightforward constructions imaginable. This is because the arguments he gives for his thesis will apply everywhere or nowhere. Whether or not there are *any* such *universal* reasons, I believe (along with Quine's critics) that his *articulated* reasons never do apply.[8] As regards the present relativistic effort, as well as more generally, it is instructive to explain why this is so.

Quine's main argument for indeterminacy may be understood in connection with his leading illustration. This case concerns the translation of a native word, 'gavagai', conspicuous in the discourse of some distant tribe. For a field linguist, the natural hypothesis is that 'gavagai' means *rabbit;* the word is used affirmatively often in the presence of such perceptually salient edible items. For Quine, the natural hypothesis has no objective claim to correctness over various alternative construals. Although it may be most convenient for the linguist to translate 'gavagai' as 'rabbit', there is just as much truth in the idea, no more and no less, that it should be translated by our 'rabbit stage' or, again, by our 'undetached rabbit part' or by any of a number of other English locutions.

Every time there is a rabbit to be affirmed in behavior, there is also, after all, an undetached rabbit part, a rabbit stage, and some other metaphysically related items. At least, let us suppose with Quine that this is so. If that is so, then behavior most directly pertaining to 'gavagai' will not discriminate among the suggested translations. Will some other linguistic behavior, less directly pertinent, serve to favor just one translation?

Each translation of 'gavagai' carries with it correlative translations of connecting jungle locutions. For the linguist's 'rabbit', a simple jungle expression comes out as our copula, a form of 'to be'. For 'rabbit stage', that simple expression translates as, say, 'are stages of the same animal'; for 'undetached rabbit part', it becomes, say, 'is part of the same animal as'. By making enough appropriate adjustments, a variety of complete translation manuals can be produced. None of these, Quine contends, is objectively better or truer than any of the others.

Quine's contention is based, first and foremost, upon the idea that a speaker's behavior is what (ultimately) controls which translations are appropriate for his words. That idea does seem correct and has been guiding our own efforts. But his contention is based, further, on a more specific idea, which can be vaguely put like this: that the control of behavior on translation is quite *direct.* That seems wrong.

Translating the language of some people is, in effect, ascribing a certain language to them, notably the semantic aspect of their language. This involves, in turn, attributing to them a certain semantic understanding. Any given hypothesis that they have a certain semantic understanding, if it is well founded, will belong to some overall theory that purports to explain their behavior. Many of the theory's other statements will concern the psychology of the people, of which their semantic understanding is a part. Other psychological statements will concern their various beliefs about things, their modes of perception and of inference, how perception and inference lead to their beliefs, how beliefs and other psychological states lead to their behavior.

We speak in line with how we perceive, believe, desire, and act; so does everyone else. If I ascribe a word meaning *undetached rabbit part* to your *basic vocabulary* and do not ascribe one meaning *rabbit,* then in effect I am ascribing to you a psychology heavily involved with the numerous inconspicuous parts of more salient things. Especially if you are a jungle primitive, not some learned metaphysician, this makes your thinking, and even your behavior, appear extraordinary, ridiculous, perhaps even insane.

Suppose you want a rabbit for a pet. In that thought connects with language, your desires should be most simply expressed in your own words. If I translate your 'gavagai' as indicated, I will ascribe to you some such desire as wanting to have undetached rabbit parts around to fondle. But this makes your thinking, which is, in fact, sane and commonplace, seem either mad or else exceptionally complex, like the technical thought of a metaphysician.

As it flows from your beliefs, desires, and other psychological states, your purposive behavior should be described compatibly, in your own words. Suppose you believe you can easily get a rabbit by bartering for one. That is what you do; some behavior you can simply report. On the proposed translation, your behavior is to be characterized, even by you, as being (somewhat) like this: You bartered for a normally arranged and functioning group of undetached rabbit parts. This makes your behavior seem that of some biology *collector,* whereas your primitive society, we may presume, is quite devoid of any such hobbies.

It is not merely a matter of convenience that people have short expressions, simple syntactically and semantically, for what is conspicuous to them. Nor is it just a matter of convenience that we translate others' words along those lines. It is also, and very much so, a matter of making sense of behavior. Because language connects with behavior by way of an inclusive psychology, I must assign you a *comparatively* simple semantics. And, to make *any* semantic complexity plausible for you, I must, as we have been arguing throughout, effect a *compensating gain* in simplicity for much of your psychology. On Quine's argument, however, I am to make your semantics more complex *along with* my making your psychology more complicated: instead of evening everything out at zero, so to speak, Quine's alternative translation doubles the total complexity for you.

Perhaps our points may be clarified in connection with an example from the philosophical literature, amplified appropriately. Suppose that you are a person just like me, a qualitatively identical duplicate, but far away and without relevant causal relations with my society. Assume, as Max Black has in another connection,[9] that your planet, call it Dual Earth, is on the other side of a plane that bisects a mirror universe. Then, even your whole galaxy is qualitatively identical to mine. Eventually, you make a trip here, while I take a mirroring journey to Dual Earth. Each of us begins to translate.

We should each translate our respective terms simply and the same; just as we both will do. I should translate your 'rabbit' as meaning *rabbit*, as equivalent to my 'rabbit'. If our brains are qualitatively the same, and also our (brain-directed) behaviors, why should I make you out to be otherwise, to be any more complex. If Quine's argument were right, then I might just as well translate your 'rabbit' as 'undetached rabbit part'. Indeed, I might just as correctly translate it as 'stage of an undetached part of an instance of rabbithood' or as some still longer and more complex "behaviorally equivalent expression." There is no limit on the allowable complexity or length, nor even any on the way simpler parts will combine in the whole, as with a standard recursion. On Quine's argument, I need then only posit an exceptionally complex translation for your 'to be' and for your other expressions in an appropriately compensating fashion. But, with a brain just like mine, how would you quickly process the logically complex, wholly unconstrained material I am imparting to your structure of thought, so that you might, without undue delay, behave appropriately with respect to quick rabbits? For that matter, with only such a limited brain, how could I behave adaptively with so much conceptual baggage?

Our translations, in effect our semantic theories, must accord with the rest of what we hold true, not only psychology but neurology, information theory, sociology, and more. No part makes much sense apart from the whole of our view of things. In a word, our accounts of linguistic behavior, as of anything else in the world, should be *holistic*.

On a holistic approach to behavior, only 'rabbit', among the alternatives Quine suggests, makes sense of the native's use of 'gavagai'. Neither does there seem any other equally good translation of that word, not yet suggested. So, Quine's argument for indeterminacy fails if a suitably holistic approach is accepted.

As regards the indeterminacy of human natural languages, Quine is right, but not for the right reason. In that Quine is perhaps the foremost advocate of a holistic approach to explanation, there is a certain irony in this situation.

When we accept Quine's holism, we reject the direct and exclusive tie he posits between behavior and semantics. Then, we look for a way to make compensatory adjustments, not where Quine does, but in the more inclusive sort of behavioral account we must allow. The relativistically related approaches of contextualism and invariantism provide, I believe, one way of projecting such adjustments in the large. For that reason, they provide appropriate arguments for much of Quine's indeterminacy thesis, a holistic line of reasoning toward much of his semantic view.

In our discussion of Quine, we have followed, though perhaps not very closely, a course charted by previous critics, notably by Putnam.[10] Then, we have taken further steps in several directions, particularly in our consequent agreement with much of Quine's thesis of indeterminacy. So, in the end, our position is not very far removed from Quine's. Moreover, the *attitude toward* the relativity theses central to the present work is to be much the same as Quine's was, or at least appeared to be, toward his celebrated thesis. To Putnam, at least, Quine's attitude appears quite cautious indeed:

> . . . The position of the real Quine . . . allows that [further] con-
> straints may be well motivated, motivated by just the considerations . . .
> that are operative in the growth and development of physical theory. . . .
> [But] even the discovery/stipulation of such further constraints as might
> prove well motivated would still not determine a unique translation. There
> would still be, he expects, some indeterminacy of translation.
>
> Note, then, that on Quine's view the indeterminacy of translation is a
> hypothesis, not something of which Quine claims to have a logical or
> mathematical proof.[11]

Was Quine's attitude toward his indeterminacy thesis actually as tentative as Putnam states; was his thesis regarded as no more than a hypothesis? I do not know. But we can say that, whether or not it was, it should have been. So should our own attitude now be a highly tentative one toward our proposals of semantic and philosophical relativity. Emphatically, I consider these relativity theses as no more than hypotheses, not as propositions for which we now, or soon will, have overwhelming or even compelling reason. Throughout this work, and even at its end, we will not strive to embrace these proposals or to commit our belief to them. Rather, we will only endeavor to entertain, as a serious option and a geniune possibility, the idea that these hypotheses just might provide a rather accurate and even illuminating perspective on the relations among language, thought, reality, and philosophy. My aim, then, and I hope the reader's, too, is a truly modest one. We are to be of an open mind, and increasingly so, toward certain suggestions: that our relativities might be more accurate, and more illuminating, than those propositions of commonsense thinking (whichever precisely they are) to which they stand in (some sort of) opposition; moreover, that this might be so even if those commonsense propositions not only now do but perhaps always will command our belief automatically.

II

Aspects of
Semantic Relativity

Our argument for semantic relativity requires that invariantism be a viable semantic approach. This approach, as we will increasingly observe, is less in accord with our commonsense ascriptions than is contextualism. In a limited sense or way, that makes it rational, as we will argue, to prefer our habitual contextualism to the invariantist view. But this limited rationality of preference will not be grounded in any greater truth of contextualism, only in its habitual employment. As far as any more objective considerations go, it is our hypothesis, the two views are on a par. This parity appears to hold across a wide domain of phenomena. Therefore, our hypothesis of semantic relativity, as we will observe, appears to have rather wide application.

1. Contrasting Groups of Expressions

Certain expressions in our language have one sort of semantic role; others have another. When examining one group of expressions, we may note contrasts between its members and those of another group. Then, it may be tempting to think that only one of our two approaches, say, invariantism, can adequately account for the differences. But, on our hypothesis of semantic relativity, that would be an erroneous judgment.

Alternatively, one may notice that, despite their interesting contrasts, there are important similarities between the two groups. When focusing on these similarities, one may be tempted to think that only one of our two approaches, say, contextualism, can adequately account for them. But, on that same relativity thesis, that would also be a mistaken inference, for, as the hypothesis will have things, there is enough room for accommodating psychological description

21

so that either semantic approach can explain both the contrasts and the similarities.

Many of our predicates are typical *vague* terms. With many of these, their function is simply to express, vaguely, *to what degree* an object of our discourse has a certain property (in a suitably general sense of 'property').

With most words that appear to be of this sort, there is little room for alternative interpretation in this most general matter: 'red', 'short', 'bumpy', 'confident', 'doubtful'. But, with some apparently vague words, the situation is more complex: 'flat', 'empty', 'safe', 'dry', 'certain'. In some respects, these latter words are semantically similar to the previous group; in other ways, they are semantically unalike. How are we best to describe these differences and these similarities?

An invariantist may well emphasize the differences, apparently at the expense of the similarities: True enough, he says, we use 'flat' to get across the idea of how flat something is, but that is really the idea of *how close* to being absolutely flat it is. For 'flat', like 'certain', 'safe', and so on, always expresses an absolute limit beyond the various degrees of mere approximation to it. This is a very different matter from our use of 'bumpy'. When we are getting across the idea of how bumpy something is, that is all there is to the matter; for there is no (coherent) idea of how close something is to being absolutely bumpy, or even any idea of being absolutely bumpy. Words like 'bumpy' really are vague words, while words like 'flat' only appear to be vague but actually are not. The latter, which we will call *absolute terms*, perform (most of) the functions for us that the genuinely vague words do; but, not being vague, they do so only in a rather indirect fashion.

In line with this, the invariantist may continue, we may notice the contradictions we hear with sentences like 'That is flat, but that other is flatter' and 'He is certain of this, but more certain of that'. Once one is at the limit, the invariantist explains, there cannot be any going beyond. We notice no such logical discomfort with 'That is bumpy, but that other is bumpier' or with 'He is doubtful (confident) of this, but more doubtful (confident) of that'. Since no limit is at hand, there is no difficulty with going further.

There is not much doubt that 'flat' and fellows contrast with 'bumpy' and company. And the invariantist account just indicated as appropriate only for the first group is, I suggest, one way of describing this contrast. Along with that, the invariantist can say, too, some things about the similarities: Both sorts of expressions typically serve to bring to mind relevant matters of degree, vaguely expressed and conceived: the degree to which a field is close to being perfectly flat. The invariantist account is appropriate to the phenomena; it is relevantly complete. So, one might conclude, as I once did, that *only* such an account can be adequate.[1] But that would be, I now suggest, an erroneous conclusion, perhaps the result of taking too narrow a view.

A contextualist need not be insensitive to the contrasts between these two sorts of terms. But he will emphasize the similarities, apparently at the expense of those appreciated contrasts. The contextualist will then insist that *all* of the terms really are vague terms, the absolute terms included: It is just that, for a contextualist, these latter are a rather *special sort* of vague term, with special *context-sensitive* semantic features. By thinking along these lines, a contextualist may, as David Lewis has done, conclude that the *only* adequate semantics of 'flat' and 'certain' is a *contextualist* semantics:

> Peter Unger has argued that hardly anything is flat. Take something you claim is flat; he will find something else and get you to agree that it is even flatter. You think the pavement is flat—but how can you deny that your desk is flatter? But "flat" is an *absolute term:* it is inconsistent to say that something is flatter than something that is flat. . . .

> Some might dispute Unger's premise that "flat" is an absolute term; but on that score it seems to me that Unger is right. What he says is inconsistent does indeed sound that way. . . .

> The right response to Unger is that he is changing the score on you. When he says that the desk is flatter than the pavement, what he says is acceptable only under raised standards of precision. . . . Since what he says requires varied standards, the standards accommodatingly rise. Then it is no longer true enough that the pavement is flat. That does not alter the fact that it *was* true enough *in its original context.* "The desk is flatter than the pavement" said under varied standards does not contradict "The pavement is flat" said under unvaried standards, any more than "It is morning" said in the morning contradicts "It is afternoon" said in the afternoon. . . . Unger . . . can indeed create an unusual context in which hardly anything can acceptably be called "flat," but he has not thereby cast any discredit on the more usual contexts in which lower standards of precision are in force.

> In parallel fashion Unger observes, I think correctly, that "certain" is an absolute term; from this he argues that hardly ever is anyone certain of anything. A parallel response is in order. . . . It is no fault in a context that we can move out of it.[2]

As regards such terms as 'flat' and 'certain', Lewis does note that there is *something distinctive* in their semantics. Against my (early) invariantist treatment of these terms, however, he holds that the special semantic features of these expressions are quite limited in scope: Even as 'bumpy' and 'doubtful' are *vague* terms, so, too, are 'flat' and 'certain'. The difference is just that the latter are a *special sort of vague term with contextually assigned limits for their temporary operation.*

Lewis holds that this contextualist treatment is supported by, perhaps even required by, the ability we have to accommodate our thought, and our attendant behavior, to many changes of context. In Lewis's terminology, this is our ability to alter, and to keep track of, the "conversational score." But does our "knowing the score" favor the idea that only a language with contextualist semantics is the one to be attributed to us? I do not think so.

Along the lines Lewis indicates, we may appropriately attribute such a language to us English speakers. Then, we will describe our knowing the score in the terms Lewis employs. But perhaps we may also attribute, just as appropriately, a language with invariantist semantics. Then, we will just have to employ correlative modes of semantic and psychological description.

For an invariantist, how do we keep track of how (nearly) flat something must be to be acceptably called 'flat' at a given stage in a conversation? We do this, the invariantist says, by keeping track of how close a thing must be to a certain absolute standard in order to be acceptably called 'flat'. That standard, unconsciously in mind, is the state of being such that nothing could possibly be flatter. True enough, at a given conversational stage, a surface is acceptably called 'flat' when it measures up to the temporary standard for flatness then relevant. But that temporarily relevant standard is reckoned in relation to the invariant absolute one, which is the only standard our word 'certain' itself directly expresses.

On the invariantist interpretation of our behavior, we will have ideas of these contextually relevant standards as *contextually acceptable departures* from absolute governing limits. Now, it is true that certain other contextually relevant standards, those in use for uncontroversially vague words, will be more directly employed, without reference to any absolute limits. That is, to be sure, a simpler business. But, then, both invariantists and contextualists admit that matters are *somehow* simpler with typical vague terms, like 'bumpy', for which no problematic contradictions ever even seem to be encountered.

The contextualist has the greater complexity of the facts about 'flat' accounted for by way of a more complex semantics for the term itself. It has all of the relevant complex features of typical vague terms and, in addition, the complexities involved in the assignment of temporarily operative limits on appropriate ranges. Along with this, there are quite complex psychological acts of understanding the semantics of these terms.

The invariantist also strives to account for the complexity of the facts about our absolute terms, but while always assigning a simple semantics to the terms themselves. Accordingly, he supposes there to be complex psychological processes that are not directly involved in the semantic understanding of words like 'flat'.

On the invariantist's account, apparently as good as any, it is by way of these associated processes that our complex uses of 'flat' and fellows are to be described and the adaptive sensitivity of our guiding thoughts to be accounted. What do our rules of accommodation do for us with these special expressions?

They allow us to create, and to keep track of, the acceptability, and the unacceptability, of various departures from some simple, invariant semantic conditions.

The changing course of a conversation may be quite complex indeed; the participants move from context to context, creating or accepting new ones, destroying or ignoring the old. As our adaptive behavior attests, we keep track of all of this well enough. How so? Just as with less dynamic explanatory quesions, there is, we hypothesize, no determinate answer. A contextualist description can be given in terms of which our linguistic and cognitive movement can be well enough explained. But there can also be given, apparently with equal explanatory propriety, an invariantist description.

2. Statements, Beliefs, and Truth-values

With the sentences focused upon so far, say, 'That field is flat', the semantic "disagreements" in each case revolve around a certain component word, in this case around 'flat'. With various other sentences relevant to our discussion, the locus of relativity is not so conveniently circumscribed. There is thus a certain diversity in the linguistic matters encompassed by our relativity thesis.

Suppose that we are attending a small conference in New York City, and the people whom we are now most interested in discussing are those expected at the meeting. Perhaps all but five checked in today. In light of this, someone may ask, "How many are in town?" In response to those words, someone else may reply, "Well, three people came to New York this morning." What *question* was actually asked here? And what *statement* was made in way of reply? An invariantist will give one answer, a contextualist another.

For the contextualist, the question asked was this: *Of the relevant group of entities,* how many are in town (in New York)? The sounds uttered do not come very close to expressing the question. Perhaps the interrogative *sentence* used does. But, in that case, the sounds will not fully express the sentence. The question, and maybe even the sentence, has a hidden, implicit, silent operator "up front" that delimits the relevant reference class. Understanding the question, and maybe even the sentence, involves grasping this operator and its import. Or, if he does not say quite this, the contextualist will take some such complex semantic line.

His line regarding the statement made will follow suit: *Of the relevant group of entities,* three people came to New York this morning. Understanding the statement, and maybe even the declarative sentence, involves grasping this implicit restriction of domain and interpreting everything else accordingly.

For the invariantist, neither the question asked nor the statement made, nor the sentences used, has any such implicit restriction. Such a restriction enters our thought only at another place, one removed from semantic grasping and evaluation. Of course, the effects achieved will be contextually relevant. First, the audience gets to focus on this idea: The questioner wants to learn how many *of the relevant group of entities* are in New York. The replier then makes his statement in a way most conducive to satisfying this appreciated desire. How so? He says something that gets the questioner to focus on this idea: Of the relevant group of entities, three arrived in New York this morning. But, the invariantist stresses, the means employed nowhere involved any complex *semantic* operation or understanding.

Let us think about what *statement* the replier *made*. For the invariantist, this statement will be a false one, at any rate *not true:* The statement has it that (exactly) *three* people came to New York this morning, while in truth many thousands then came to this town.[3] For the invariantist, such a result is not unusual: The making of a false statement quite often occurs when ordinarily we would take it that only a truth was spoken. This is a paradoxical consequence. Now, in *some* way, we may count this against invariantism. But in *what* way might we properly do that? In particular, is it a way that undermines semantic relativity?

In the first place, we should notice that this particular paradox concerns statements made, not beliefs held. In the case at hand, the invariantist may well allow the replier to believe only that many thousands of people arrived in New York at the relevant time; he is not required to say that the replier actually believed that exactly three people arrived there then. All this seems plausible enough. What the invariantist will then say is this: In making his (brief) statement, the replier did *not directly express* his most relevant belief in the matter. Rather, he said something easier and more convenient to say. For the invariantist, this often happens: We often say what is easiest rather than what directly expresses our most relevant beliefs.

In the second place, it is not simply that the invariantist often stands between us and the truth, even in the domain of statement making. Rather, the general matter is more complex: the truth-values he would assign are *other than* those we would most ordinarily propose. True enough, in most such discrepant cases, he assigns falsity instead of truth, but sometimes he assigns *truth in place of (presumed) falsity*. Invariantism is not as simplistic as one might first suppose.

Suppose someone is asked to be on the lookout for boats. After an hour during which no boats were in his view, he is asked, "Have you seen any boats?" He replies deceitfully by saying "Yes, I've seen quite a few boats; I can't recall exactly how many." What statement or statements has he then made?

As everyone may agree, our replier has gotten his questioner to *focus on* the proposition that, during *the past hour,* he has seen quite a few boats. For the contextualist, this is what the man said to be so. Given the particulars, the *contextualist* has the replier saying something false, *not* true.

According to a typical enough invariantist interpretation, however, this respondent did say something *true,* despite his relevantly successful deception. As almost everyone has, he *has* seen quite a few boats—if not at the time of interest, then at some time(s) in the past. (Moreover, just as we cannot, he cannot recall exactly how many boats he has seen; he spoke the literal truth about that, also.) In cases like this, it is the invariantist, not the contextualist, who has our statements be in line with the truth.

As the foregoing example sentences might also be used to illustrate, there are several possibilities for positioning in these matters. One might be a contextualist, for instance, with regard to sentences with the simple past tense and an invariantist for corresponding sentences in the past perfect. Then, one may evaluate as true a sentence like 'Bud ate three hot dogs' and evaluate as untrue 'Bud has eaten three hot dogs'. If one takes this somewhat complex compromise position, one will have yet to decide which position to take on such sentences as 'Bud did eat three hot dogs'. So, there are invariantists and invariantists and contextualists of various shades and degrees: How one distributes the semantics and the pragmatics for certain sentences need not be determined by one's position on certain other sentences. But, of course, in the present work we are mainly interested in the contrasting treatments possible for our language. Accordingly, we often use the labels for our two *isms* as though they denote monolithic positions, with little room for overlap or compromise. This is a harmless enough expedient: Our invariantist, we may conveniently say, will treat each of the three sentences above in the same strict semantic way; he will look for (merely) pragmatic differences signaled by the different strings of words.[4]

In general, the relation of our two approaches to our relevant statements' truth-values is as remarked: The contextualist has these truth-values be *those we ordinarily presume,* while the invariantist has them be *otherwise.* What this means is that contextualism is a semantic approach more in keeping with (the dominant aspects of) our commonsense view of things.

3. Logic and Meaning

A man points at an ordinary field and says, quite felicitously, 'That field is flat'. The earth there is, by any very strict standard, at least a bit uneven or irregular. For the contextualist, the sentence, as then used, is nonetheless true (or expresses a truth). For the invariantist, it is false. For the relativist, however, neither of these clear options is open. On the relativity hypothesis, we are not using the sentence to make any statement with determinate truth-value. What is the relativist to say, then, about the status of such sentences?

Various options are open. First, at least relative to most uses, a relativist can assign such sentences some third, nonclassical truth-value, say, *indeterminate,* or *indefinite.* Or, if he would have each item with any truth-value be classically valued, a relativist can say that these sentences lack truth-values. They have an appearance common to many sentences that are true and to many others that are false, but they themselves are neither. So, second, one might opt for a truth-value gap here.

Some will not like either of the options exhibited; they like their truth-values all classical and their fields of bearers all gapless. To those of this inclination, the following may appeal: Many sentences that look to express genuine propositions actually do not. For a sentence to succeed in doing this, it must have determinate semantics, at least as used on some particular occasion. Thus, a third relativistic option: The sentence 'That field is flat', as well as many philosophically more interesting sentences, will often, if not always, fail to express any genuine proposition. Now, saying that we often fail to express any genuine proposition with typical uses of such ordinary sentences, and many of them philosophically interesting ones, may at first seem badly paradoxical. But some of the sting is taken out, I suggest, when we realize that 'proposition' is here being used in an especially artful sense, a sense in which no propositions can be at all indefinite, a sense in which all must be determinately true or else determinately false.

As far as I can tell, any of these options is viable enough. In all events, none will peculiarly help or hinder our relativity hypotheses. Rather, the appropriateness of these conjectures depends on other matters, as we have been endeavoring to clarify.

As is obvious enough, there is a certain broad similarity between the relativist and the traditional skeptic: Both hold that the truth-value situation of many things we say or express will be other than we ordinarily assume. But within this broad similarity crucial differences appear at once: What are we supposed to *do* about such troublesome words as 'flat', let alone those of greater philosophical importance, such as 'certain'? For the traditional skeptic, since the expression in question has a fully determinate semantics, there is nothing to do, except perhaps to change the subject of inquiry. For the relativist, however, the semantic conditions are not yet all laid down; there is still room for conventional stipulation, in one direction or in another.

Without violating the meaning of, say, 'flat', we may endow it with a more fully determinate sense than it yet has had. With any such indeterminate term, we may adopt certain conventions that will endow it with more exhaustive and articulate semantic conditions. For example, we may adopt such conventions as will have our 'flat' be evaluated semantically only in a contextually varying, sensitive fashion. Or, alternatively, we may impose such other conventions as will have the word be evaluated without any relation to context, thus always the same. Along with all of the conventions so far governing the use of any such word, it is our hypothesis, there is still ample room for either course of adopting conventions.

I will not attempt to spell out the details of either sort of additional conventions, nor will I try to detail how our behavior is to be regulated by either. But let me venture to sketch a broad difference between the propensities toward linguistic behavior that would be variously induced. The venture is, admittedly, speculative.

Should we adopt appropriate fully contextual conventions, a skeptical attempt to interrupt a conversation might have terribly little appeal, if any, and perhaps would be brushed aside as irrelevant, almost as an attempt to change the subject entirely. In other words, one who should "challenge" the claim of *flatness$_c$* for a road by pointing out with a magnifying glass many tiny irregularities might be taken, quite immediately, to be as far from the claimant's subject, or very nearly as far, as happens with the following: Someone "rebuts" a claim to the effect that it is raining by pointing out that in some area irrelevant to the context, perhaps the Sahara Desert, no rain is falling anywhere now. Likewise, a claim to *know$_c$* as "challenged" by reference to possible deceit by a Cartesian demon might be decisively felt to be, and declared to be, receiving no real challenge at all, not even one of theoretical interest. Thus, there might eventually occur some such broad shift in our linguistic behavior.

Through the adoption of invariantist conventions, there can occur, we might surmise, a broad shift to opposite effect. Such "challenges" as just discussed might, in such an event, be taken as absolutely genuine challenges and, indeed, as literally successful, but with respect to *flatness$_i$* and *knowing$_i$*. The people whose statements were challenged would, in this scenario, almost immediately acknowledge the falsity of their remarks and admit that they were speaking only very loosely, of course, much as though using figures of speech. They would admit that a road, or a field, was no more really *flat$_i$* than, as we now admit, a certain person was really going to *die of embarrassment.* They would admit that a person no more *knew$_i$* that another was angry, and do so just about as readily, as we now admit a certain angry person was never really about to *hit the ceiling.* There might, therefore, upon the adoption of certain other, "more stringent" conventions, eventuate some such quite different broad shift in our linguistic behavior.

As things stand, our hypothesis says, we have not yet adopted either sort of dimly envisaged additional conventions. Perhaps that is why, or is one of the reasons why, our actual linguistic behavior, covert as well as overt, is an uneasy mixture of the comfortably settled response patterns just sketched in outline. So much for my speculative venture.

In any event, let us suppose that, whatever their exact nature and behavioral import, we have gone ahead and adopted fully adequate contextual(ist) conventions for 'flat', 'certain', 'know', and other problematic expressions; in that way we will have resolved their problematic indeterminacy. As regards semantics, what will be the result? We will now have words that differ semantically from those we used before. Since the words in question remain numerically the same, we will have *changed the meaning* of many of our words. This we needed to do in order to use these words so commonly in sentences that express simple positive truths about the world.

According to traditional skeptics, we will have to do that, to change meaning, in order to use, say, 'know', to express such truths. In this general way, the relativist is like the traditional skeptic. But within the broad commonality an important difference arises: For the skeptic, since the old meaning gave fully determinate semantics, the new meaning will go against, or contradict, the old. For the relativist, in contrast, the new meaning will not contradict the old.

For the relativist, but not the skeptic, our newly determinate sentences will not be so very different, in their semantic conditions, from the old sentences disputed at such length. Viewed in this light, our relativity hypotheses can be seen to provide a compromise of sorts between more standard positions that are more directly opposed.

4. Sortalism

Each of our two semantic approaches achieves, I suggest, very considerable, and exactly equal, overall simplicity in accounting for our adaptive behavior. On the one hand, invariantism keeps semantics as simple as can be, paying a psychological price elsewhere for so doing. Contextualism allows complex semantics, but highly flexible and sensitive semantics, so that associated inference is kept to a sweet and simple minimum. Is there a way of combining the best features of both, so as to achieve an account superior to either? I cannot see how this is possible. In an undogmatic spirit, I suggest the hypothesis that there is no such superior position.

That there be semantic approaches superior to both of those sketched here is, although apparently unlikely, quite compatible with relativity, both philosophical, of course, and even semantic. What is not consistent with semantic relativity, it should be noted, is this: That there be a *single best* semantic approach doing more than any other for a single best behavioral explanatory account. But the *reason* I offer for *taking seriously* semantic relativity, and thus also philosophical relativity, is this: That there does not seem to be *even one* semantic approach better than invariantism *and not even one* better than contextualism. The situation of multiple superior approaches, just vaguely envisaged, is no genuine road to relativity, as far as we can tell. For us, there is not even one semantic approach that is better than, or even as good as, either of the two we have been examining.

In a recent paper on some of the present topics, Fred Dretske appears to differ.[5] In criticism of my early invariantist line on "absolute terms," Dretske seems to offer a very substantial compromise, more than a relativist is able to allow. At least at first glance, he seems to give quite a bit to the invariantist (skeptic), to grant quite a lot to the suggestions of semantic stringency. At the same time, he seems to acknowledge the semantic sensitivity to situation that graces the position of our contextualist:

> . . . I want to . . . illuminate our concept of knowledge by showing how this absolute idea can, despite its absoluteness, remain sensitive to the shifting interests, concerns and factors influencing its everyday application. In short, I want to explore the way, and the extent to which, this absolute notion exhibits a degree of contextual relativity in its ordinary use. . . .

> I have . . . my agreement with Unger. Knowledge *is* an absolute concept. . . . Unlike Unger, though, I do not derive skeptical conclusions from this fact. I will happily admit that *flat* is an absolute concept, and roughly, in the way Unger says it is, but I do not think this shows that nothing is really flat. For although nothing can be flat if it has *any* bumps and irregularities, what *counts* as a bump or irregularity depends on the type of surface being described.

> . . . a road can be perfectly flat even though one can *feel* and *see* irregularities in its surface, irregularities which, were they to be found on the surface of, say, a mirror would mean that the mirror's surface was not really flat. Large mice are not large animals and flat roads are not necessarily flat surfaces.[6]

If available, such a substantial compromise would be an appealing alternative. Has Dretske presented us, however, with a viable option at all? I do not think so.

For Dretske, the semantic application of an absolute term, a term such as 'know', 'flat', 'empty', 'certain', or 'safe', is to be assessed in a linguistic environment that, at least implicitly, connects the term to a sortal noun, to an expression that stands for, or demarcates, a *sort*, or a *type*, of things: The words 'That is flat' said of a *road* are to be evaluated differently than those words said of a *mirror*, the words 'road' and 'mirror' standing for things of different sorts or types. Naturally enough, we may call this third position *sortalism*.

Sortalism differs from contextualism: According to sortalism, there is no very direct connection with a user's temporary interests and the truth-value of what he says with those expressions in the relevant range. Unlike the contextualist, the sortalist recognizes as having relevant semantic import only those enduring widespread interests of ours that are already reflected in the categorial words of our common language.

Sortalism also differs from invariantism: For the invariantist, we can evaluate the sentence 'That is flat', on a typical use, without needing to know or to specify what sort of thing *that* is. For the sortalist, such free-floating evaluation is impossible. What is "flat enough" to be a flat *road* is not "flat enough" to be a flat *mirror*. Where they serve as adjectives, the sortalist seems to say, absolute terms function as *attributive*, not predicative, adjectives. According to sortalism, the invariantist makes the mistake of ignoring this linguistic distinction. Skeptics about flatness, let alone knowledge, get much of their (confused) appeal by getting us to ignore the need for sortal specification.

Trying to effect a compromise, the sortalist does find *some* common ground with the invariantist. Once a sort of thing is specified, standards suited for things of that sort always must be met. Otherwise, a statement predicating an absolute property to a thing will be false, much as the invariantist so very often has it. Dretske's clearest example here is that of a *bottle* that has one drop of liquor (or wine) in it, not *no drops* at all. Suppose someone says of this *bottle*, even referring to it as a bottle, that it is *empty*. For sortalists like Dretske, a bond with invariantism is clear: "No one is going to quarrel with this description since all the relevant implications (e.g., we can't make another martini) are true. But the claim itself is false."[7] Those are the words that, in fact, close (the body of) Dretske's essay. A contextualist, it should be clear, would not let matters rest there, not by a long shot. He would attribute such semantics to our relevant terms, here notably to 'empty', as would have us saying what is true so much more of the time.

I believe it to be clear enough that sortalism is inferior both to invariantism and to contextualism. Before we examine the matter, however, it is worth noting that relativity does not require anything as strong as that result. For semantic relativity, all that is required is that sortalism *not be better* than invariantism or than contextualism. Indeed, if it is as good an approach as (either of) these, that would be fuel for the relativist's flames, the more power to him. Against a *relativist*, then, the burden of argument is on sortalism.

Let us examine the position of sortalism. In the first place, it can often yield contradictory semantic evaluations where no contradictions seem to exist and where adaptive thought would have trouble handling such intrusive inconsistencies (then needing to manage such apparently needless complexities). Consider, as a fair enough sample, Dretske's own contrasting sortal terms: 'road' and 'mirror'. Now consider as well a stainless steel object, both a road and a mirror, used for filming automobile commercials and for getting cars from certain parts of the General Motors main complex to others. (The case is imaginary but, I take it, entirely consistent.) Now, suppose that this object has less in the way of bumps and irregularities than (almost) any other road but more than (almost) any other mirror. Someone says of the thing, "That is flat." Because the thing is a road, what the speaker said is true. Because it is a mirror, what he said is not true. This is a contradiction. How do we resolve the inconsistency so as to proceed with adaptive thought and behavior in a context at hand? Sortalism requires us to import some special psychological mechanisms, both ad hoc and complex.

Let us switch from 'flat' to 'safe', from one absolute term to another, emotionally more charged. We always have in mind as an object a certain *vault*, an object of that kind. Indeed, not only is the object always of this same sort, it is always the same (wholly or largely unchanging) vault. But our contexts differ, from time to time, and from speaker to speaker. In one conversation, someone says, "That vault is safe"; the salient concern is the protection for a few days of a few thousand dollars from usual thievery. In another conversation, someone says, "That vault is *not* safe." But here the concern is the protection for some indefinitely long period of many millions of dollars worth of rare gems from clever international jewel thieves. Because the sortal used is the same both times (and the worldly situation of the vault itself is exactly the same or relevantly similar), sortalism has us evaluate what is said the second time as inconsistent with the first remark. For adaptive thought and behavior, however, we need to treat the statements differently, if not semantically then at least on some other level; we should have a systematic guide available to such an effect. Without becoming unduly complex, sortalism provides us with no such adaptive mechanism.

In marked contrast, both contextualism and invariantism neatly incorporate relatively simple procedures for us to attain adaptive behavior. The sortalist is an inefficient middleman; he asks for his share of the semantic spoils, a rather handsome share, but pays back little or nothing toward appropriate action and its fitting explanation. As a contributor to behavioral explanation, his semantics is worse than useless. Among semantic approaches in the field, the sortalist's is, I submit, readily eliminated.

By noting their contrast with sortalism, with a representative attempt at substantial compromise, we appreciate the explanatory simplicity and power of our sketched semantic approaches. Both invariantism and contextualism are, it appears, exceptionally good semantic components for a theory of behavior. The trouble is, if we must regard it as a problem, that neither of them is any better than the other. That is, at least, the way these matters do appear, thus seeming to support, in just the way indicated, our hypothesis of semantic relativity.

This relativity, we can continue to notice, may apply to a very wide range of expressions, with interesting logical connections among various locutions in the range. As Dretske serves to remind us, it can apply just as much to 'without any bumps and irregularities' as it does to 'flat'. Despite certain initial appearances to the contrary, some of which favor invariantism and others of which speak for contextualism, the former expression, just as the latter, may be semantically indeterminate.

5. Extreme Semantic Approaches

We have noted, examined, and finally rejected a semantic approach, sortalism, that means to steer a path somewhere between contextualism and invariantism. The question naturally arises, at this point if not earlier, whether there might be any tenable semantic approach more extreme than those we have been finding agreeable: either more severely invariant than the view we have been calling invariantism or more highly contextual than the view we have been calling contextualism. Now, although we might contemplate such extreme semantic approaches, I do not think they will prove tenable.

A most extreme approach in the invariantist direction might be this one, call it *superinvariantism:* Each of our (declarative) sentences means the same thing as, and expresses the same propositions as, every one of the others. Then, every one of them might express a single grand acknowledged truth, perhaps, that the universe exists, which is a more pleasant prospect than having us always assert a much more meager truth, say, that one and one are two, or an obvious false-hood, say, that nothing exists. Still, any of these alternatives is formally available.[8]

For the superinvariantist, everything is in the pragmatics, nothing is in the semantics, for a proper explanation of adaptive behavior. No matter how grand the truth expressed, no matter whether it be absolutely true, it will (almost) always be quite irrelevant to the context in which talk, thought, and behavior take place. When someone utters the sentence "Your gloves are in my car," what he asserts is simply, say, that the universe exists, a proposition that, even when believed, will not help you at all to get your gloves. There must be some inordinately complex associated psychology attributed to you by way of which you move from the proposition grasped, the thought as to the universe's exis-tence, to that pertaining to context, the thought as to the whereabouts of your gloves. In brief, this is the extreme approach of superinvariantism.

A most extreme approach in the contextualist direction might be this one, call it *supercontextualism:* Every time there is a shift of attended proposition, there is an appropriate meaning for the sentence used to effect that focus of thought. Consider again the sentence, 'He is closer to fifty years of age than to forty', which, as ordinarily used, suggests the proposition that his age is *between* fifty and forty. For the supercontextualist, there will be a meaning of that sentence according to which that proposition is logically entailed by what is said. Or, perhaps, this approach will have the *only proposition expressed,* by a most typical utterance, be the thought that his age is between forty and fifty. Now, in certain unusual contexts, the proposition brought to focus by an utterance of the sentence will actually be the thought that the numerical differ-ence between the number of his years and the number fifty is greater than the difference between the number of his years and the number forty, whether or not the number of his years is between the other two numbers. As it is used on those occasions, rather rare, the sentence will mean this other thing (that which it seems always to mean).

For the supercontextualist, then, nothing (or almost nothing) will be allowed in pragmatics. Semantics will be all encompassing, or so near to that as makes no difference. If 'closer' must often take on (so much of) the meaning of 'between', so be it.

Now, it seems to me perfectly obvious that superinvariantism is an absolutely untenable semantic approach toward a group of speakers even remotely like ourselves, nowhere near what objective truth there is in the matter. And it seems nearly as obvious that supercontextualism is also untenable. But *why* are these approaches objectively so inadequate? Without being very illuminating, and putting matters very roughly, the answer seems to be this: Any account of our adaptive behavior, if it is even to have a fair amount of truth in it, must include at least a fairly rich semantics and also at least a fairly rich pragmatics. (And the two must dovetail in some appropriate way so that, oftentimes, a substantial contribution to explanation is made by each.) With both invariantism and contextualism, I suggest, this situation does obtain. With both superinvariantism and supercontextualism, it fails to obtain.

It seems to me an important question for future research to say more precisely what is wrong with these extreme approaches. But this question need not detain us here, however important it is from other perspectives.

In closing this brief section, let me make a purely logical point. Suppose that, contrary to all that is plausible, these extreme approaches are, somehow, objectively no worse than either invariantism or contextualism. That will not, it should be clear, entail the failure of semantic relativity. On the contrary, the relativity hypothesis would, in such an unlikely eventuality, then be more widely applicable than we have been arguing, not without any application at all.

6. The Relativity and the Rationality of Contextualism

As we noted, contextualism is a semantic approach that, more than its chief competitor, invariantism, is in accord with (the dominant aspects of) our commonsense view of things. Contextualism is more deeply involved with more of our developed intellectual habits. Now, we may take this as being, in *some* way, a point in favor of contextualism and against invariantism. But this is not the sort of point, or the sort of way, that undermines the hypothesis of semantic relativity.

The relativity thesis does not imply that these two appraoches should be equally preferred by us. On the contrary, it fully allows that we might well prefer contextualism and even be rational in doing so, at least in some limited sense or way. What the hypothesis denies is that the basis of this preference will be that the one approach better accords with objective facts than does the other.

The fact that invariantist assignments of truth-values are so frequently surprising points to our habitual preference for contextualism over invariantism. But, as the relativity hypothesis implies, these assignments concern only *proposed* explanatory properties for *posited* explanatory entities—assignments of truth-values for statements. These are not objective predications for acknowledged things in the world. As far as objective reality goes, we are reasonably free to posit what statements we will, and then what truth-values we assign, providing that we make *compensatory psychological posits* elsewhere in our explanatory story. Now, owing to our contextualist habits of attribution, the psychological posits that the invariantist requires are also strange and surprising, just as are the semantic posits of his total view. But none of this strangeness need indicate any greater objective truth for the more habitual mode of attribution or for the more commonsensical judgments encouraged thereby.

Suppose that two procedures lead to different conclusions regarding matters of objective fact. One of the procedures might be our own, involved in our linguistic and cognitive practices; the other, if not hypothetical, will be peculiar to some quite alien society. Then, there arises the problem of justifying our own procedure as rational, at least as more rational for us to follow. One approach to this problem is to claim that it is simply the "entrenchment" of the first procedure in our society, the past and present employment of its terms and modes of attribution, that grounds the rationality of our preference for it. This is a sort of methodological conservatism. Such a conservatism does have some plausibility. But it is controversial that it can adequately account for, or justify, the presumed rationality of our own procedures and expectations in these matters of objective fact.

An outstanding example of such a controversial claim is in reference to Nelson Goodman's two languages with concomitant inference patterns: our own, with 'blue' and 'green', and an alien one, with "temporally indexed" 'grue' and 'bleen'.[9] In this situation, we and the presumed aliens have different expectations regarding certain matters of objective fact, even observable, concrete fact: They expect certain stones to be a certain color when observed at certain future times; we expect those objects to be otherwise. Intuitively, and very vaguely, we have the idea that the aliens are irrational in their procedures because they are counterinductive in them, while we, for being inductive, are rational in ours. Is this vague thought correct? Maybe it is, and maybe it is not. If it is, then there is more to our own personal rationality than just our sticking with that procedure we have already got. In situations like Goodman's, where there are disagreements as to objective facts, it is controversial that methodological conservatism can do much to explain our own expectations as being rational ones.

In the present case, however, there appears no disagreement as to objective facts at all. So says our hypothesis of semantic relativity. If that is so, then a very *mild* conservatism may, without much controversy, explain the rationality for us of our contextualist ways: If two equally coherent procedures lead to equivalent expectations concerning all (possible) objective facts and depart only as regards conventional assumptions used in explanation of the facts, then it is rational to prefer the one with which one is already comfortable, adept, and familiar. This relatively uncontroversial justification of contextualism, and of our associated commonsense thoughts about our statements, is, it seems to me, a point in favor of hypothesizing semantic relativity.

No doubt there are factors that explain why we are in fact contextualists, why we have accepted this approach and not the other. These are likely to involve considerations as to what habit patterns are more natural or more convenient for us, which will better foster improved social relations among beings like ourselves, and so on. Toward so many ends, it is productive for us to "take folks at their word," not to question their veracity; so that is how we treat each other. But however that may be, such socially helpful considerations do not, I think, confute semantic relativity. At least I cannot see how they undermine the hypothesis.

7. The Appeal of Invariantism

We have noted a key attraction of contextualism, which it retains even in the face of semantic relativity: On that view, but not on the approach of invariantism, the truth-values of ordinarily made statements come out the way we ordinarily believe them to do. And, in particular, they will usually come out as true, since, ordinarily, we believe such statements usually to be true. But, while most of the attraction is thus on the side of our habitual contextualism, not all of it is: Invariantism, too, has its own distinctive appeal for us.

The appeal of invariantism arises with its most definitive feature: On that approach, the semantics of the relevant expressions is as *simple* as might be supposed with any plausibility. All of us, I suggest, have the belief, or at least the tendency to believe, that the semantics of most ordinary expressions, including those discussed here, is a rather simple affair.

As regards certain expressions to which our relativity hypothesis seems to apply, our belief in simple semantics has a philosophically interesting consequence, also implicitly accepted. This is our belief that the semantics of these expressions is appropriately *independent*, that the conditions do not depend on the contextual interests of those happening to use the terms on a particular occasion. Let me illustrate with some examples; two will be reconsidered, one will be introduced.

First, we reconsider 'flat'. Now, whatever we may implicitly believe to the contrary, we think this term properly applies to a surface just in virtue of features of *that surface's shape, not* in virtue of quite *removed* features, such as the *interests in* the surface *taken by people* who happen to be talking and thinking about it in a *certain conversation.* We think, then, that it cannot be true to say of a given surface at *one* time that it *is* flat and at *another* that it is *not, unless there has occurred a change in the surface's shape itself.* And, at a given time, it cannot be true for *one* person to say of a certain surface that it *is* flat but *not* true for *another* person to say that about the surface. The truth-value of their statements cannot depend, we tend to think, on the interests of the people involved in two simultaneous but distant and unconnected conversations about the very same surface as it is at that particular time.

We turn to another familiar example, the expression of personal certainty. Whatever implicit beliefs we might harbor to the opposite effect, we do believe that it cannot be true of one person that he *is* certain of something, say, that twelve times twelve is one hundred and forty-four, but *not* true of another person unless there is some real difference in the psychological states of *those two people* or in the relations *they* bear to the proposition. The truth-values cannot depend, we presume, on the interests of some *third parties* who, on one occasion or another, may happen to converse about the people and the proposition in question.

Now for a new example to illustrate the same general point: Whatever else we may also believe, we tend to think that (almost all) singular causal judgments are independent of our specific conversational interests. Suppose, for example, that an auto accident has taken place and there are two conversations regarding it, each interchange removed from the other. In one conversation, the participants are road engineers; in the other, they are people in charge of issuing drivers' licenses. In the first interchange, someone says that what caused the accident was the inadequate banking of the road at the curve. In the other, someone else says that the drunken driving of the man at the convertible's wheel caused the accident. Well, which was it? From our external viewpoint, we seem pressured to adjudicate. That is, these judgments of causality *appear* to contradict each other. But suppose that, in fact, they do not. Then, the truth-conditions of each judgment will depend, not just on objective relations among events and objects on the highway, but also on the (temporary) interests of whomever happens to be discussing the events in question. Contrary to our presumption, our causal judgments will not then be relevantly independent propositions.

On an invariantist account of 'flat', 'certain', and 'cause', the semantics of these terms will be not only as simple as we generally suppose but also independent. This is quite in line with our commonsense beliefs about these terms and about the statements in which they enter. For a contextualist, however, none of this can be so. In these regards, then, it is invariantism, and not contextualism, that is in accord with common sense.

On many matters, common sense is inconsistent; we do not actually have our unreflective thoughts so perfectly in line all the time. So, in particular, it is with matters of semantics: On the one hand, we believe that most statements ordinarily made with 'flat' and fellows are true; on the other, we believe that the semantics of these terms and statements is not only relevantly simple but relevantly independent, or interest-free. Common sense would have it both ways, but that is impossible. This point, of which I am fairly confident, does not require any relativity hypothesis to hold.

In that common sense is ambivalent in these matters, it is an oversimplification to say, as we have done, that commonsense semantics is contextualist semantics. But it is not a harmful exaggeration. For the common beliefs favoring contextualism are much *stronger* than those favoring the opposite approach. We believe more strongly that most of our ordinary statements with these expressions are true, less strongly that their semantics is simple and independent. On the *whole,* then, our habitual modes of ascription are contextualist, not invariantist.

Nonetheless, insofar as it flies in the face of our belief in simple, independent semantics, contextualism engenders *something* of a paradox, even when viewed from within our commonsense perspective: How can the matter of whether a given surface is *flat,* in contradistinction to, say, whether it is suitable for our croquet game, depend upon the interests in that surface taken by those who happen to converse about it? This appears to go against our better judgment: If it does not go against the strongest, most influential aspect of common sense, perhaps it goes against its best or truest aspect.

Can such a paradox of contextualism undermine it as a tenable approach? If so, then we will be left with invariantism alone, and our hypothesis of semantic relativity will be jeopardized, at least for these expressions. But I do not think that contextualism, or relativity, will so easily fall.

Why do we believe that our ordinary locutions must, by and large, be semantically independent of our own interests and depend solely on features and items that are relevantly external? Partly because our own interests are so close to us that they go unnoticed unless explicitly mentioned, while in the cases at hand the (contextualist) reference to our perspective is only an implicit one. But most of the explanation, I think, can be traced to other sources.

As regards almost any genuine subject matter of our discussions, we must have *some* expressions available that *are* independent, whose conditions are free of the temporary interests of a particular user. Or, at least, we have a strong tendency to believe this to be so. So, in particular, we must have *some* objective way of describing the shapes of various surfaces and objects, *some* terms for independently indicating the "confidence level" of people with respect to propositions, *some* suitably independent terms for indicating the causal relations, if any, that obtain between certain events.

Let us suppose that this general claim, so appealing to our belief, is true. Even so, it may be that 'flat' is, despite appearances to the contrary, not among our independent terms for surface shape. And it may be that 'certain' is not part of our independent, interest-free vocabulary for confidence levels. Finally, despite appearances, it may even be that 'cause' is not one of our expressions for independently describing what passes as the causal order. Even if all of this is so, we may still have other expressions, of course, to do the job of interest-free description.

According to the contextualist, our actual situation is as follows: Either we have no interest-free expressions at all for these subject matters, or, as is somewhat more appealing, we do have some but they are not the terms that come to mind (perhaps they are only certain complex concatenations of common words, quite unobvious to us and possibly even inaccessible). According to the invariantist, that is not the situation; rather, we do have interest-free terms, as we seem to require, and, moreover, they are just the terms that come to mind as fitting the bill. According to semantic relativity, of course, there is no fact of the matter here as to what actually is our linguistic situation.

Intuitively, this present matter is as the invariantist claims, not as claimed by either the contextualist or the relativity hypothesis. For, as observed, 'flat', 'certain', and 'cause' do seem to be among our independent expressions. But, I suggest, this appearance need not be decisive.

We tend to think, perhaps even as a part of common sense, that the semantics of our ordinary words is, not only a rather simple affair, and often independent of interests, but also something *readily accessible.* We have an intuitive understanding of such familiar words; we just grasp their simple meanings and that is that. But it may well be, I suggest, that the understanding of semantic conditions is not nearly so simple as this part of common sense would have it.

The semantics to be assigned to an expression comes as part of an overall theory of the behavior of those speaking the language in which that expression has a place. Because an appropriate theory is not readily accessible, the semantics of many of our ordinary expressions is not, I suggest, so accessible. Among those familiar terms whose semantics is not accessible, we may conjecture, will be those to which our relativity hypothesis applies. So, even though the intuitive inclination toward the invariantist claim of independent treatments for 'flat', 'certain', and 'cause' is strong (whatever the details of the treatments), that inclination may be misleading.[10]

8. General Sentences, Conversational Interests, and Contexts of Utterance

We have been examining certain sentences, for example, 'That field is flat', that may usefully be called *particular,* in contrast to *general.* Let us now try to say something about more general sentences such as 'Many fields are flat' and 'Tabletops are flat'. To the extent that we can do this, our relativistic discussion will be that much more comprehensive.

Suppose someone utters the general sentence "Tabletops are flat." Generally, though not universally, there will be some interests involving surface shape provided by the context and pertaining to the utterance. What are some contexts in which, or with respect to which, such interests obtain?

One such context is this: We are planning a large cocktail party and are wondering whether, without further adjustments, we will have enough places about the house for people to place their glasses. We are making a list of all the *sorts* of places available and of the items of each listed sort. But, somehow, we have left out the most obvious places. One of us pipes up with the observation that "tabletops are flat." Since we have five tables, their tops, along with the twenty-four items of the other nine types of available objects, will provide us with enough places for our expected guests to put down their glasses.

Another such context is this: We are trying to teach our toddler the correct use of 'flat' in connection with objects' surfaces, to teach him as much of the relevant meaning as we can. We then might say, "Many fields are flat," and "Tabletops are flat." (Doubtless, we will also use some particular sentences here, mixing the types of sentences enough to keep the lesson interesting enough to be learned.)

In the first case, the interest most relevant in the context is apparent enough, and so it is clear enough that there is some relevant interest. But what about the second case? Is there any relevant interest there at all according to which 'flat' and sentences containing 'flat' may be semantically evaluated (on the contextualist's approach)? I am not sure of the matter, but I think there is. Very roughly put, the interest is this: giving the audience a good enough idea of what sorts of things are, oftentimes, acceptably regarded as flat in our society. Good enough for what? Good enough for the young audience to function successfully, to satisfy his or her desires, in the situations, social and otherwise, that someone in our society is apt to encounter.

If this is right, as seems plausible enough, then the contextualist can have the general sentences uttered be true or express true propositions in the second case as well as in the first. And, in all likelihood, he can do the same for almost any relevant general sentence in almost any context of utterance. The invariantist will, of course, have matters run quite oppositely throughout. Since he seems able to give a story that, overall, is just as effective an explanation, all of these cases will, it appears, conform to the hypothesis of semantic relativity.

Then, there are what we may call *negative general* sentences, for example, 'Tabletops are *not* flat'. Might a contextualist sometimes evaluate such a sentence as true? He could if there were a context in which a relevant interest is involved. I suppose that a discussion in a course devoted to Euclidean geometry might well provide such a context. When the surfaces of a Euclidean cube are discussed, it is important, for the progression of the course, to distinguish, with respect to the absence of shape irregularities, those items from such mere physical things as tabletops. To answer to these educational interests, the surfaces in question must be such that nothing could ever possibly be flatter than they are: Here, sufficient closeness is, or amounts to, zero distance from that severe absolute standard. In this matter, of course, there will appear no difference between the approaches of contextualism and invariantism.

In that relevant interests will be so often generated from context, utterances of general sentences will be systematically well treated both by contextualist and invariantist. With these contexts and utterances in mind, then, we have that many more instances of semantic relativity. But, though quite infrequently, there are utterances of sentences, whether general or particular, in which no relevant interest is provided. What happens on such occasions, especially as viewed by our relativity hypothesis?

Suppose one utters the sentence "Tabletops are flat" as a sample sentence for grammatical parsing; no interest in surface shape is anywhere in the neighborhood. Two questions arise: First, what is a plausible treatment of this uttered sentence with respect to semantics? Second, whatever such a treatment, we have an unreflective tendency to hear the sentence as expressing a truth, so what is a plausible treatment of this tendency? Let us take these questions in reverse order.

With no helpful context to guide us, why are we still willing to assent, on the whole, to the sentence 'Tabletops are flat'? Although there is no decisive answer, we may conjecture that, most of the time, a hearer is apt to think of the sentence as though it were uttered in a context in which surface shape mattered and in which the interests regarding such shape were themselves rather ordinary. Then, the thought focused on, by way of such a most typical utterance, is something like this: that, for the purposes typically most relevant contextually, tabletops are sufficiently close to being absolutely flat. And, as we reckon things, that attended proposition will actually be true. Since this plausible conjecture is available to both the contextualist and the invariantist, the question of our tendency to hear truth expressed here favors neither view. Accordingly, it appears to do no harm to the hypothesis of semantic relativity.

What, now, for semantic treatment of the sentence itself, even as thus uttered? For a contextualist, this following line seems most inviting: In a context in which no interests in surface shape are provided, one who utters "Tabletops are flat" will fail to make any statement or to express any proposition. Therefore, there will be nothing in such an interest-free situation actually susceptible of any truth-value, nothing true or false (or anywhere in between). The sentence, as then uttered, will not be evaluated as true and, perhaps, not evaluated semantically at all.

This treatment is, I think, formally available to an invariantist. But another line is more appropriate to his position. For simplicity's sake, an invariantist may well prefer to have propositions abound. Then, because of the molecular composition of actual tables, with any utterance whatever of 'Tabletops are flat', an invariantist may have the speaker express something false. (With any utterance of 'Euclidean planes are flat', he may have the speaker express a truth.)

As far as I can tell, neither of these two treatments is objectively preferable to the other; each fits very well into a different sort of explanatory account of behavior, and each account is as good as the other. If this is so, then even for the most marginal cases of linguistic behavior, the situation is relativistic.

9. The Compatible Vagueness of Semantic and Pragmatic Terms

Tenacious as it may now seem, how does our hypothesis of semantic relativity first gain any foothold? The quagmire of vagueness, so characteristic of our language, may be the appropriate ground. Let me explain.

We distinguish between various aspects or features of various of our expressions: Some are *semantic* aspects, others are *pragmatic*. Typically, the former are more closely tied to the expressions themselves; the latter concern more accidental, removed features. All of this is extremely vague. Some of the vagueness is a defect, an incompleteness, only of my characterization. But a substantial remainder may concern the distinction itself.

In terms of this apparently vague distinction, there is much that the contextualist and the invariantist may take as common coin: Both can say that there is a lot of pragmatic understanding and a lot of semantic understanding. But, within a certain range, there may be room for different allocations: The contextualist has the semantic understanding amount to *more* than the invariantist would have, and the pragmatic amount to *less*. By way of this terminology, the hypothesis of relativity says that what semantics is properly assigned to a given population is *relative to* what pragmatics is assigned to those people, and vice versa.

How does this work out? We may take it that 'semantic' and 'pragmatic', as well as near synonyms of either, are *vague* expressions. Moreover, and perhaps more important, they each will apply to many expressions that are themselves vague. There is, then, a vagueness in 'semantic' and in various semantic terms, and there is also a vagueness, or elasticity, in 'pragmatic' and in various pragmatic expressions. Now, the first group of elasticities might be compatible with the second group in such a way that room is created for a multiplicity of explanatory descriptions, involving terms from both groups, of people's experience and behavior. If that is so, then one appropriate description might give 'semantic' and company a somewhat larger range of application, and another description, objectively neither better nor worse, may give less there while giving more to the pragmatic group.

These considerations give us a picture of our language in which a feature is a significant vagueness in quite a few explanatory terms with a matching, or compatible, vagueness in various other explanatory expressions. It is this feature that explains how there might be the relativity that our hypothesis postulates. But, what of this higher-level explanatory feature? Is it an *objective fact* of our language that it contains these expressions with their suitably compatible elasticities? I am uncertain.

On the assumption that there is any substantial determinacy in matters of semantics for natural languages, it seems reasonable to suppose that these features are objectively part of English: There seems no proper construal of the language we actually now employ on which 'semantic' and any expressions falling under it—'meaning', 'sense', 'reference', 'application', 'sentence', 'statement', 'word', and 'understanding the meaning of a word'—are anything but quite vague. And the same seems true for 'pragmatic' and its group—'suggestion', 'belief', 'inference', and so on. Moreover, on any reasonable interpretation of English, on any reasonable posit of a language for our society, the conditions for each group of expressions will have a significant relation to that for the other. We will understand what sentences we may have, and what they mean, only in some (perhaps vaguely described) relation to the beliefs we might have "involving" our sentences (and to the inferences we are disposed to make in relation to our system of sentences and beliefs). Given all this vagueness, and all these interconnections, it is hard to think that the former will not attend the latter. And, if that is so, then, finally, it is quite plausible that this vagueness will attend these interconnections in such a way as to promote semantic relativity. Given this reasoning, it appears that our claimed relativity is indeed an objective fact of our own linguistic situation.

The reasoning is plausible, not conclusive. Let us suppose that it is in error. If it is, then how should we treat the hypothesis of semantic relativity? Must we abandon the proposal and firmly embrace the natural, unreflective idea of our linguistic situation as objectively determinate, with just one semantics and one pragmatics as uniquely most appropriate to explain our behavior? We might do that, I suppose, but we need not. In a relativistic spirit, let me propose what now seems a more interesting possibility.

As far as I can see, any lack of determinacy, or of objectivity, in our account of compatible elasticities will only mean *even more* relativity than we have so far articulated, not no relativity at all. Statements that our language has such and such a range of allowable semantic interpretations, with such and such a range of correlative pragmatic employments, will themselves be true only relative to certain higher-order explanatory posits, each (group) of which will exclude the others. From a relativistic perspective, we can then say this: There will be nothing objective to decide matters between any two such higher-order alternatives.

Suppose that nothing concerning relevantly low levels of language has gone awry in our arguments for the hypothesis of semantic relativity. That is, suppose that up until this present section, all has gone well, or well enough, for this hypothesis. Then, if we must abandon our relativity as most simply construed, the likely perspective will be an extended relativity hypothesis, not the commonly unreflective idea of determinate semantics. From this perspective, there may be an *infinite hierarchy of arbitrary assumptions to be made* in order to resolve conventionally an infinity of compatible elasticities. Perhaps all of this relativity can only be "indicated," and then only relative to certain arbitrary assumptions. Then, let us admit, or pretend, that we have just accepted some such assumptions, whatever their content. Perhaps we have, by way of that acceptance, indicated the infinitely complex relativity that is our linguistic situation.

III

A Relativistic Approach
to Some Philosophical Problems

We proceed to apply our relativistic approach to some philosophical problems. In each case, the treatment will proceed along the same general lines: First, look for some expressions that are important for a statement of the problem in question. Then, try to see how the thesis of semantic relativity might apply to the expressions encountered. We will argue that, for each problem studied, an invariantist can assign a semantics to the philosophically important terms that is comfortable to a skeptical view on the problem, and a contextualist can, with equal propriety, assign a semantics that is comfortable to the commonsense position on the problem, antithetical to the skeptic's position. On our hypothesis, since there is nothing to decide between the two assignments, the problems under review are insoluble: Although we might prefer one alleged solution to the other, that of common sense to that of skepticism, there is nothing to decide objectively in favor of either position.

1. A Problem of Knowledge

In the course of conversations, we claim to know many things about the world. The skeptic denies these claims, saying that we actually know nothing to be so or, at most, very little. These denials are motivated by arguments.

Many skeptical arguments take the following general form. The skeptic conjures up some propositions, each of which fairly obviously conflicts with what one claims to know to be true. If one really knows what one claims, the skeptic says, one must be in a position to rule out as untrue these logically conflicting propositions. But it seems that one cannot rule out those propositions

46

noted by the skeptic. So, the skeptic concludes, one does not really know what one claims to know.

Arguments of this form have a considerable pull on almost everyone acquainted with them. Also, there is a considerable resistance to them that, almost always, eventually outweighs that pull. How is this to be accounted for?

In an ordinary conversation, when I say to you, "John knows there is milk on the rug," I get us to accept, among other things, some such complex contextually sensitive idea as this: Among the propositions logically conflicting with 'There is milk on the rug', John is in a position to rule out, according to standards for ruling out that are relevant to current context, all those conflictors that are *relevant* competitors. What competitors are relevant? Like the standards for ruling out taken as being in force, that, too, depends on the context and, thus, on our interests in the situation. Therefore, this thought, upon which we are brought to focus, is relevant to context in two ways. These ways are not wholly unrelated.

What I am proposing here must, I am afraid, remain somewhat vague even after my attempts at clarification, which follow.

To begin, I do not mean 'ruling out' to imply any articulation of reasons for regarding as untrue any proposition that may thus be so regarded. Nor does it imply, even, any ability to provide any such articulation, demonstration, proof, or whatever of the falsity of the ruled out proposition. Rather, the idea is that, when a proposition is ruled out, any chance at truth for that proposition may be (appropriately) discounted or ignored.

To further matters, we might say that, when one is experiencing (in the visual modality) only a homogeneous visual field of pure blue, one is in a position to rule out, and probably will have ruled out, the proposition 'I am now visually experiencing only phenomenal red'. And, typically, one will have done so even according to a very high standard for ruling out, one rarely used in, or required by, human conversations. Perhaps according to a higher standard than even that, one is in a position to rule out 'I do not exist', especially when one is consciously thinking, more especially when one knows that one is, most especially when one is aware that the falsity of that negative proposition follows, logically and immediately, from what one then knows so directly and so certainly. In contrast, only according to a very much lower standard than either just contemplated is one in a position to rule out the proposition 'My friend Frank is at the movies' when, earlier in the day, Frank had told one that he was going to spend the evening quietly at home. Ordinarily, the standard for ruling out appropriate to conversations about spilled milk and rugs (and about knowing) will be somewhat higher than the standard just contemplated, though quite a bit lower than the two standards contemplated previously to that one.

When I say to you, 'John knows there is milk on the rug', what competitors to 'There is milk on the rug' are *relevant* ones; which need ruling out? Like the standard in force for ruling out, that, too, will depend on context, so that our behavior may be contextually adaptive. In many ordinary contexts, though by no means all of them, a relevant competitor will be that there is only some whitish water on the rug that looks like milk but is not milk. In everyday contexts, certain other competitors will never be relevant, or at most scarcely ever: For example, that any experience as of milk and rugs is caused only by an evil demon who, in that way, gets one to believe falsely about such "external" matters.

In ordinary contexts, both standards for ruling out and ranges of relevant competitors are not as great as they might be. Thus, in at least two ways, complex thought and behavior can be adaptive to ordinary contexts. Now, even though these two ways are related, there is room for divergence: In some ordinary contexts, the standard may be relatively high even while the range is not all that great: Suppose that the rug is a rather valuable antique susceptible to damage by continued exposure to old milk. Suppose, also, that it is extremely expensive to clean the rug in order to prevent such exposure. Further, suppose that the only liquids anywhere on or near the premises, the only candidates with any significant chance of being spilled on the rug, are milk and harmless whitish water. In such a case, where John may have seen the spilling, the standards for his ruling out the whitish water will be quite high, while the range of competitors is quite minimal.

On the other hand, the standards for ruling out may be rather low even while the range of competitors is extensive. Suppose the rug is a rather cheap nylon thing, easily cleaned, and, to boot, not at all likely to be spoiled by exposure to milk or any other available substance. In addition, suppose that, on the premises, a combination drugstore and luncheonette, there are many liquids available that are of a similar whitish appearance. Again, John is the most likely witness. This time, for us to find 'John knows there is milk on the rug' acceptable, we will require that John be in a position to rule out quite a few competitors to 'There is milk on the rug', but rather low standards for ruling out will be those in force.

It almost goes without saying that, in everyday contexts, the remaining two alternatives are found: Often, we both impose high standards and consider large ranges; often, both the standards set are low and the ranges considered are narrow.

Finally, we may say this about our thought as to knowledge: As the standards for ruling out get higher, other things being equal, the relevant ranges become greater; as the ranges become greater, *ceteris paribus,* the standards become higher. At the very highest point for either, we must be at the highest point for the other; we are then, but only then, beyond *ceteris paribus* considerations. So, anywhere lower down, on either isolated dimension, we are not beyond such considerations. And this often happens in everyday life. Indeed, it often happens that other things are, not only relevant, but relevantly unequal. Our two examples about the milk and the rugs were two cases of such rather common divergence.

As we have been urging, the matter must be complex: For a limitation on the range of relevant competitors to be effective in allowing knowledge, the standards in force for ruling out must be sufficiently low. Otherwise, there would be this problem: According to the *very highest standards* for ruling out, not relevant to ordinary contexts, to *rule out,* say, 'There is milk only on the floor', one would have to be in a position to rule out, as well, 'There is an evil demon deceiving one into false belief as to whether or not there is milk only on the floor'. But, even according to fairly low standards for ruling out, one cannot, it seems, rule out this latter proposition; I cannot, you cannot, and, in particular, John cannot.[1] For adaptive thought, then, there must be an appropriate relationship between the two contextual features: It is only a certain (somewhat modest) range of competitors that is to be ruled out, and even they are to be ruled out only in a certain (somewhat modest) way, only according to a certain (somewhat modest) standard.

It is in this overall situation of adaptive thought that the skeptic about knowledge can make compelling arguments.[2] He may begin his negative moves in either of two main ways logically related to each other: He may start by bringing in competitors not usually deemed relevant or even envisioned at all. Or he may start by suggesting, quite compellingly, a movement toward higher standards for ruling out. Eventually, either of these will begin to involve the other; the skeptic may then seem to have things both ways at once. Although it means some repetition of certain points recently made, let me spell this out in just a bit of detail. For purposes of illustration, let a fledgling skeptic start by introducing novel competitors.

As is familiar, the competitors even a fledgling skeptic proposes are of the sort that, in ordinary conversations, we would (almost) never deem relevant. In relation to our examples, he might propose these conflicting propositions: There is, for John and perhaps for us, too, only part of a *perpetual* dream here, the part in which one dreams some milk is on a rug, while in reality there is nothing to it; there is only deceptive experience, induced by an evil demon, as of a real situation of milk on a rug but nothing real to answer.

When such "all-encompassing" competitors are at issue, the range of competitors will be at the maximum: all (rather obviously conflicting) competitors are fair game. And at that point, as we have said, the standards for ruling out are at their highest, too. So, the game is then set up for the skeptic to win overwhelmingly.

Suppose, contrary to our statement of convergence, that there are (sometimes) low standards for ruling out in force while the proposition to be ruled out is, for example, that an evil demon is deceiving in the matter (so that the range of competitors is at a maximum). Well, as we previously noted, even according to fairly low standards for ruling out, *such* a competitor is one the alleged knower *cannot* rule out. So, the supposition of low standards here will be to no avail in any case. We might as well suppose, as we did and as seems more intuitive, that when the range is so great the standards must be so high.

Now, let us take the skeptic's other main approach: The skeptic begins by urging us to raise the standards for ruling out; we go along, further and further, until the highest standards are in force. Does John know there is milk on the rug? With such high standards in force, it seems that, for John to know, he must be in a position to rule out (just about) any proposition conflicting with 'There is milk on the rug', in particular, even 'There is an evil demon deceiving me into false belief in the matter of whether or not there is milk on the rug'. But this proposition, it seemed, could not be ruled out even if standards for so doing were fairly low (which is not to say absolutely minimal). So, again, John does not know what was claimed for him.

A serious skeptic, no mere fledgling, says we never know anything about the world, or at least something nearly as sweeping. Is what he says true? That depends on, among other things, the meaning, or the semantics, of 'know': For the skeptic, an invariantist account of the semantics of 'know' will prove most congenial. On such a semantics, sentences of the form 'S knows that p' will have as a logically necessary condition some such severe proposition as this: S is in a position to rule out as untrue, according to a single invariant standard for ruling out that can never be transcended, *all propositions* that are (at least fairly obviously) logically incompatible with p (not just those competitors relevant for this or that person to consider, in this or that context).[3] Semantically, the invariantist thus contends, it makes no difference what alternatives to p are relevant for those involved with a given use of a given sentence of this form. The skeptic will embrace invariantism: If this sort of semantics gives the right account of such sentences, then, in particular, a claimed knower must always be in a position to rule out (according to the highest standard for so doing) various machinations of Cartesian demons, whether or not those involved with the making and the hearing of a particular knowledge claim take such considerations to be germane.

On a contextualist account of 'knows', in contrast, sentences for knowledge claims will have more complex, context-sensitive semantics: These sentences, the contextualist holds, will *directly express* contextually relevant thoughts or propositions. So, they will often, not never, express truths; they will do so depending not only on what (somewhat modest) standards for ruling out are relevant but also depending on what (restricted range of) competitors are relevant. Both the standards and the range, as regards their relevance, will vary with the context.

Now, it is very plausible to suppose that, *given* the falsity of such propositions as 'There's an evil demon deceiving in the matter', certain people can rule out, according to suitably modest standards for so doing, such competitors as 'There is only whitish water on the rug'. If a contextualist semantics for 'know' is right and the situation is as ordinarily presumed, then such a person might well know that there is milk on the rug. Contextualism hinders the skeptic and aids the commonsense epistemologist.

Invariantism favors skepticism about knowledge; contextualism favors the opposite, more commonsensical view. These are the main lines for us to notice. Still, within this large picture, there may well be certain smaller points that are worth noticing. It seems to be so.

An invariantist account of 'know' will *directly* give the day to skepticism about knowledge, at least to a fairly extreme form of that view. A contextualist account of 'know' will not, however, give the day to common sense *quite* so directly: Even if there is always an implicit reference to the *relevance* of alternatives, the skeptic can claim, for example, that, as a matter of fact, all (logically possible) alternatives always *are* relevant. Or, at least, he might claim that all those propositions are relevant that can be seen to be (logically imcompatible) alternatives by a reasonably good reasoner (if not the claimed knower). But, with nothing much to support it, even the less ambitious of these skeptical claims seems just something for the skeptic to say for want of anything more compelling or substantial.

Once it is thought that a contextualist account of 'know' does specify some contextually sensitive conditions that are fully determinate for the term, the skeptic has a very long and hard row to hoe. He must try to create contexts in which the very highest standards are enforced, and then he must sustain those contexts. Now, perhaps the skeptic can do this for some fleeting moments, in certain highly rarified philosophical discussions. David Lewis seems to think that this occurs frequently enough. Perhaps it does, but I am uncertain.

Even if he can sometimes create such effective philosophical contexts that high standards of exclusion will be temporarily in force for 'know' (and often for 'flat', too), the skeptic then has the problem of *maintaining* these contexts and of extending their standards to other, less rarified, situations in which more practical concerns affect matters of what is relevant. In an excellent recent paper on this subject, Jonathan Adler argues, in effect, that these extensions are always possible, or almost always.[4] Although the considerations Adler adduces are logically powerful, their psychological force is not greatly compelling. And, since Adler is neither our president nor our king, few will create contexts along the stringent lines he recommends. Hence, almost all of the contexts we do face daily, and the statements as to knowledge we make therein, will, if contextualism is accepted, be evaluated according to low standards for ruling out and, what amounts to the same, in relation to a restricted range of competitors. If contextualism provides the correct semantics for 'know', then most of our knowledge claims will, presumably, be evaluated as true, the position of common sense in the matter. Accordingly, even if the route to it is somewhat indirect, a contextualist semantics for 'know', and for related expressions, will almost certainly mean a widespread victory for commonsense epistemology. So, as we have said, the main lines of dispute are those already noted.

Here is a related way of noting the (apparent) disagreement over knowledge claims generated by our two semantic approaches: An invariantist appears to note many contradictions between ordinary statements about who knows what. In one context, someone says, "John knows there is milk on the rug; Fred told him there is." In another, someone says, "John doesn't know there is milk on the rug; for all he knows, Fred could have been lying." For the invariantist, these apparent contradictions are genuine ones. Not so for the contextualist: The context of the knowledge claim may have, and probably did have, lower standards for what alternatives must be excluded; those were the standards then relevant. The context of the knowledge denial had higher standards relevant. Because the different standards affect the statements made and affect the assignment of truth-values, both the earlier claim and the later denial may be true. The same point can be made, of course, just in a somewhat different way, in terms of the range, or ranges, of relevant competitors. However we choose to make the point, the question remains: Are we to grant truth for invariantism, and thus for skepticism, or are we to think only contextualism, and thus common sense, is correct in these matters?

Which semantics is correct? On our relativity hypothesis, neither is objectively more proper. The acknowledged facts are these: We do keep track well enough of which people are in what cognitive positions relative to which propositions and, in consulting, behave accordingly; moreover, our talk with 'know' and cognates appropriately alters our adaptive inventories of consultants. But, with apparently equal propriety, the two semantic approaches can variously explain, or account for, the relation between the useful noises and our tendencies toward consultant behavior. Because he helps himself to the appropriate pragmatic psychological complications, the invariantist can explain the relation via his simple semantics for 'know', so helpful to the skeptic. Without those complications, the contextualist can also explain the acknowledged relation, in a manner neither better nor worse, via the complex semantics so comfortable to common sense. Since neither semantics for 'know' is objectively more proper, neither epistemological position is correct at the expense of the other: There is no decidable issue between skepticism about knowledge and commonsense epistemology. Here, we conjecture, is a conspicuous instance of the hypothesis of philosophical relativity.

This is not, of course, our ordinary view of the matter. Commonly, we think there is a genuine issue here and, moreover, one that is overwhelmingly likely to be settled in favor of common sense, not skepticism. But a relativist can account for the popularity of these conceptions. Very briefly, he may do so as follows:

Because of the simpler, more "independently aimed" semantics of invariantism, the skeptical arguments are recurrently appealing. They seem to present us with a *somewhat credible* position and, thus, with a genuine side of a decidable issue. But, because of the happily expected truth-values that it assigns to ordinary knowledge claims, contextualism has an even *greater* appeal, and so does commonsense epistemology. The latter thus appears to be the *correct* side of the matter; thus, again, and even more so, there appears to be a determinate matter before us. Such psychological facts as these, says the relativist, and not any "greater truth" of one of the traditional positions, will explain both the recurrent temptation of skepticism and the almost universal tendency to renounce it.

Within this large area of dispute, or of apparent disagreement, there are many finer points whose proper articulation is quite difficult to achieve. Whether one is an invariantist or a contextualist, one would like a detailed account of which alternatives to which accepted propositions must be ruled out by an agent in which circumstances (so that we may most adaptively consult such an agent). In detail, how does our thinking proceed here, so that, in certain contexts, we may treat the agent as one who knows or, on the skeptical description, as one who departs from knowing to a (contextually determined) *acceptable* degree? Questions of when we count alternative hypotheses relevant and when not are subtle and difficult to articulate, whether the mechanisms of assessment are largely semantic, as the contextualist holds, or whether (almost) wholly psychological, as the invariantist skeptic would have it.[5] But the intricacies of these assessments, however challenging and intriguing, can be accommodated well enough by either of our general semantic approaches. Within the compass of either form of treatment, it appears, there is plenty of room to do so. So, in an inquiry of this generality, we need not enter into the intriguing details of our adaptive procedures.

As has been traditionally recognized, problems of knowledge and of certainty are related. This fits well with our contention that, with both problems, one or the other position is favored by this or that semantic approach: For example, as skepticism about certainty is aided by an invariantist semantics of 'certain', so skepticism about knowledge is favored by such an approach to 'know'. Perhaps the parallel can be explained by logical relations between the two terms.

In earlier writings, I argued that a logical (or necessary) condition of someone's *knowing* something to be so is that the person be *certain* of the thing. Despite some considerations that seem to go the other way, this claim still seems a likely one to me. But to others it is at least somewhat controversial.[6] What seems less controversial is this other claim: that a logical condition on the person's knowing the thing is that *the thing itself be certain*. If this is right, where does it take us?

If something is certain, then, I suggest, the situation is somewhat like this: Objective considerations exclude as being untrue any proposition incompatible with that thing; they do not rule out the thing itself but thus ensure its truth. When a person knows something, he has placed himself with respect to that thing so that he is in a position to do from his own perspective what those considerations have done from the larger objective perspective.

How certain is a particular thing? For the invariantist, the question is how close the thing is to an absolute limit, that of impersonal certainty. At this limit, objective considerations have excluded from being true, even according to a highest invariant standard, all propositions conflicting with the thing, not just those we might, in a given conversational context, consider to be relevant competitors.

Does someone know the thing? For the invariantist, he does know it only if he is at a similarly absolute limit, but one referenced from his own perspective. At this correlative limit, the person has "absolutely" excluded from being true, or is in a position to so exclude, all conflicting propositions (or at least all those he can learn about), not just those deemed relevant by people discussing his cognitive situation. In both of these related matters, the contextualist's approach is the obvious variant.

Perhaps our rough characterization of these epistemological issues gives a unified picture of them. Then, we might have a unified understanding of how our two semantic approaches contribute to the endless discussion of these traditionally related philosophical problems. (Whether or not a unified conception is at hand, there is the parallel of dialectics that encourages the search for some such idea.)

In all events, questions of knowledge and those of certainty are endlessly disputed by philosophers. It is our hypothesis (not, I think, a hopelessly implausible one) that the main reason for this lies not in the perverse confusions of the disputants but in the indeterminate nature of the questions themselves.

Although there is a lot more that could be said about problems of knowledge, and about closely related issues, we cannot here go on forever. And, anyway, from ruminative experience, my conjecture is that, however many strands we pursue and at whatever length, they will all take us back, eventually, to much the same ground as we have just gone over, ground fertile for relativity. Indeed, I will not spend even this much time or space on other problem areas, to which we shall turn almost immediately.

It is nonetheless useful, even in a work of a quite general character, to have at least one philosophical problem area treated in some detail and, so, at some length. But, also, one is probably enough. If so, then the author must make a choice.[7]

2. A Problem of Power and of Freedom

We may understand a thesis of *determinism* to say that everything that ever happens is the inevitable, fully determined outcome of facts obtaining. This is quite rough and vague, of course, but not so much as to be devoid of interesting content. For example, many will find enough content here to think that this thesis is denied by important aspects of modern physics. Many should also find enough content to recognize an issue concerning the compatibility of this thesis with judgments about what we can and cannot do, about what is within our power.

A *compatibilist* believes that, even if all occurrences are thus fully determined, there are things that we *can* do but *do not* do. An *incompatibilist*, in contrast, believes that, if determinism is correct, then there will be *nothing* that we ever can do but do not. Who is right?

Well, what is the meaning of relevant sentences with 'can' and kindred expressions? Compatibilists would seem to favor a rather liberal interpretation, while incompatibilists might suggest a stringent one. Perhaps we have here, again, an (apparent) opposition between contextualist and invariantist, whatever else there also may be in the neighborhood of this dispute.

Quite apart from large issues of determinism, there is no question but that we often *think* of what we can do in a manner that is relative to context. Typically, a conversational context does not highlight the entire history of the world or all the laws of nature so we do not often think of our actions and abilities relative to such a vast, inclusive background. For example, while riding in a train with a pianist friend, a person might ask the musician, "Can you play 'One O'clock Jump'?" The pianist may reply, "Yes, I can." The musician thus gets the questioner to think adaptively: Compatible with all the facts *then relevant to consider,* there is his playing that jazz number. Therefore, the questioner might engage this musician to play in his hotel the month after next. Adaptive behavior flows from the adaptive thought, which itself is produced by both words uttered and considerations of the context of their utterance.

When impressed by how easily we guide each other's thoughts, and thus our behavior, one may well ascribe considerations of relevance to the semantics of the words themselves, to 'can' and kindred expressions. Then, the semantics of sentences of such forms as 'X can Y', 'X is able to Y', and 'It is within X's power to Y' will all be specified along contextualist lines. Discounting the nuances that distinguish their meaning, the salient semantic condition for them all may be put like this: X's Y-ing is compossible with all the facts that are relevant to consider. And what is relevant will, of course, depend on context.[8] In our example, the lack of any piano on the train will not falsify the musician's claims, on this contextualist interpretation. For the fact that there is no piano there is then not a relevant one to consider, unlike the pertinent facts of his knowledge of the jazz repertoire. In other contexts, say, in the hotel two months later, matters of truth will be evaluated differently: The absence of a piano might then falsify.

On this liberal contextualist treatment, many ordinary judgments about what people can do but do not actually do will be true. And they will remain true even if the thesis of determinism proves correct.

But one need not be a contextualist about 'can' and other terms of ability and power; one may be an invariantist. From this alternative approach, when it is said that X can Y, the meaning, or the logically necessary condition, is this: X's Y-ing is compossible with all of the facts there are (not just those relevant to consider).

As we have said, compatibilists will be aided by a contextualist interpretation of our statements. Incompatibilists will be helped by an invariantist treatment. In terms of our example, all of the facts include the fact that no piano is on board the train and the fact that nobody could make a piano suddenly become available. Given all of the facts, and not just those relevant for the conversationalists to consider, the pianist *cannot* play "One O'clock Jump" or any number at all. And, if it *was inevitable* that there not be any piano then available, then he *could not have* then played that number; so might say our invariantist incompatibilist.

What are *all of the facts?* There is room to maneuver here, which I will not try to scrutinize, let alone to eliminate. Some can say that the facts include everything about the past but not so much, if anything, about the present or the future; others might say they include everything about the past and the present but not the future; still others may hold that they include everything about all (possible) occurrences there ever will be, future as well as present and past. Some will allow facts as to what are the laws of nature; others will not. Generally, the more facts one allows, the stronger the *form of determinism* one is prepared to acknowledge. Unless it is weak in the extreme, however, any of these forms provides a basis for at least a fairly vigorous dispute between compatibilist and incompatibilist or provides at least the appearance of such a controversy.

Many readers will, I fear, be uneasy about even the more general features of our framework here. In an attempt to set them at ease, let me make what may well be a digression: I have been assuming that, for both invariantist and contextualist, indeed, for us all, there is a semantic condition on all our terms of power and ability to this effect: If someone actually does a certain thing at a certain time, then he can (or could) do it then, he is then able to do it, and so on. We often *use* these terms, however, in a manner that appears contrary: Well aware that someone has done a certain thing and probably will again, we still say, "You *can't* do *that* (sort of thing)." We thus place attention on the adaptive thought that, if the agent does such an act, then he violates something not to be violated: some state law, rule of a game, rule of etiquette, even morality itself. The specific things not to be violated will, in a given case, be apparent enough from context.

Now, in connection with such uses, a person's doing something often will be compatible with all the facts that there are, even the facts about what *are* the rules and regulations we are *supposed* to be following. Does this show an inadequacy in our semantic framework? I do not think so. Indeed, it seems that, by way of countering such a charge, we have available at least two routes of explanation.

According to one sort of explanation, we may say that the relevant terms are ambiguous. In one sense (or set of senses), that most relevant to discussions of determinism, actual doing logically implies ability and all the rest. For such a sense, a gloss in terms of compatibility with (some range of) facts is appropriate. In other senses less relevant to our philosophical problem area, there is not this implication. Only for the latter senses will our condition fail to elucidate.

Another model of explanation, which I prefer, goes like this: Our framework provides a gloss for all the meaning to be found in the area. The problematic *uses*, in which people do things the speaker accepts as done but still says they cannot do, are treated pragmatically: We pretend with the speaker that the rules in question are rock-hard laws of nature. Then, we refuse to accept as actual, still pretense, deeds of which we are aware, or else we do something similarly ambivalent.

That is enough, I think, by way of defending the general lines of our framework. It is, I believe, a framework that, suitably adapted and interpreted, provides understanding of a variety of questions disputed in this problem area, problems that are thus seen to share a common theme. We turn, then, from these questions of power to some parallel questions of freedom.

A similar dispute between compatibilists and incompatibilists concerns the question of when, if ever, people act *freely* or of *their own free will*. Will they do so in a deterministic universe? A person does something freely, I suppose, if he does it and, moreover, was free to do it when he did. Under what conditions is a person *free to do* a certain thing? He must be *free from* a plenitude of factors, say, "constraining," "binding," "preventing" factors.

In ordinary life, how do we think about these factors? Generally, our thinking is relative to context (so that it may guide behavior adaptive to the context). A contextualist account of 'free' and 'freedom' will place these considerations of context in the semantics of the terms themselves.

On an invariantist semantics, however, *any fact that there is* may always serve to undermine one's freedom, even the most recondite or unobvious. If one's *not* doing a certain thing is the inevitable outcome of some such facts, one is not then free *to* do it. Even if we would not ordinarily have occasion to consider them, one will not be free from such a determining nexus of recondite factors: they leave no alternative but for one not to do the thing. Much as with 'can', 'able', and 'power', an invariantist approach to 'free' and 'freedom' helps incompatibilism while a contextualist approach favors compatibilism.

For us to settle objectively such issues of determinism's consequences, we must, among other things, settle the semantic issue for the family of relevant terms. But, if our hypothesis of semantic relativity applies to these locutions, as it appears to do, then no such determinate resolution will be available. Indeed, in such an event, there may be no objective disagreement between the incompatibilist philosopher and the compatibilist, who appears more strongly wedded to more commonsense thinking. That this is actually the situation here, not a wholly implausible surmise, might be another instance of philosophical relativity.

3. A Problem of Causation

There are many problems of causation that have exercised philosophers. One can be illuminated, I think, by a discussion in terms of invariantism and contextualism. I am not sure how traditionally central a problem this is, but I think it an interesting problem and one that is at least in the background of many standard discussions of causality.

We suppose that *something caused* the collision between the car and the truck. But, then, *what* caused it? Depending on the context, different singular causal judgments seem in order: The cause of the collision was the oil on the road; the movements of the inebriated truck driver caused the collision; the cause was the fact that the road was not properly banked; what caused it was the overly worn tires on the car. What is thought of, and spoken of, as *the cause* of some particular thing (event), and even as that which *causes* it, depends on contextual factors.

By way of a relatively simple sentence offered, say, 'The oil on the road caused the collision', we come to accept a relatively complex thought. For that sentence, as typically uttered, the accepted thought may run like this: Of the causal factors whose outcome was the collision, the (most) relevant (or noteworthy) was the oil on the road. But what is the meaning, or what are the truth-conditions, of the offered sentence itself?

When one tries to claim each of two things as that which caused some particular occurrence, one gets a contradiction, at least an apparent one:

> The oil on the road *caused* that accident, and the inebriated truck driver *also caused* it.

> The road's being oily *caused* the collision, *and so did* the drunk's swinging his wheel to the left.

These sentences contrast with others in which no appearance of inconsistency is sensed:

> The oil on the road was *a cause* of (was part of the cause of) that accident, and the inebriated truck driver was *also a cause* (was also part of the cause).

> The road's being oily *preceded* the collision, *and so did* the drunk's swinging his wheel to the left.

Although they may be overlooked, linguistic phenomena like these, and lots of connecting sentences as well, are quite suggestive once noticed. They all conspire to suggest an invariantist account of singular causal claims, which elsewhere I have provided in fairly considerable detail.[9] On the other hand, our behaviorally adaptive thinking does suggest a contextualist approach. Therefore, the matter is at least complex and perhaps undecidable and indeterminate.

How we evaluate singular causal judgments will depend on which semantic approach we take to these judgments or to sentences standardly expressing them. On an invariantist account, the conditions are stringent: There is an absolute and unique priority for that which causes the particular thing in question. This same priority must obtain no matter what the context in which a singular causal claim is made. Now, since two items cannot both have this priority, there is a real contradiction always expressed by sentences ascribing multiplicity of causes for any given particular event. To be sure, the invariantist advises, unless the diverse ascriptions are brought into juxtaposition, we very well may fail to notice the clash. But that is just a psychological limitation of ours, one we often can overcome easily enough. And, intuitively, there is also this to be said for the invariantist account: We have the belief that matters of what *caused* what are matters of *objective relations* among events (and perhaps other things) as these are in an external (causal) order: Generally, even if not universally, these matters, these relations, are *independent* of our own temporary conversational concerns.

On a contextualist account, there will, of course, be more complex conditions for sentences of the forms 'X caused Y' and 'X was the cause of Y', where Y is something particular. The complexity will run along some such more liberal lines as these, appropriate to the thoughts on which we focus: Among the causal factors whose outcome was Y, the (most) relevant (or noteworthy) one is X. What is (most) relevant, or (most) noteworthy, presumably will be determined by facts pertaining to the context of sentence use. Now, with such a complex, sensitive, and liberal semantics, there will be no real conflict, but only an apparent one, between any two of the causal judgments about our particular highway collision. One will get a contradiction only when one tries to *combine* two such sentences into a *single utterance.* For then one will be giving the very highest degree of contextual relevance, thus the uniquely highest relevant priority, both to one candidate (causal) factor and to another one.

What is there to be said for such a contextualist approach to causal semantics, which makes causal judgments seem more matters of our own current concerns and less matters of objective relations? One enormously attractive feature is this: On such an account, almost all of our singular causal judgments can, and perhaps most of them will, come out as true.

The apparent competition between the semantic approaches underlies the philosophical problem of causation to which I was referring. On the invariantist account of singular causal sentences, there is a genuine clash between two ordinary judgments that each attribute a different cause as responsible for the same particular outcome. Implicitly adopting and urging such an invariantist approach, a causal skeptic can raise a troublesome issue: In any ordinary case, there is no objective reason, in the causal order itself, to prefer a given causal judgment, citing one particular causal factor, over each of several others that may be offered to a similar, but competing, effect: For the highway collision, as an example, any two of the factors cited might well be as important as one likes. (Just to begin, if one removes either and holds the rest as fixed as possible, one gets no collision.) When something is said to *cause* some particular happening, however, it cannot have such worthy competitors. Now, perhaps what caused the accident was the totality of causally connected prior events or else something equally grand. Or, perhaps, nothing really *caused* the accident. But, in any case, what are *ordinarily cited* as things that cause *never do cause* other things. At the very most, they are only some causal factors, within a much larger causing totality, that we happen to take as currently remarkable. Our actual judgments are (almost) all untrue.

An invariantist account of singular causal statements thus encourages a form of causal skepticism. Without such a semantics available, the appeal of that skepticism withers away. Which approach is more accurate as a semantics of our relevant causal sentences, the invariantist or the contextualist? Perhaps, semantic relativity suggests, neither is. Which position is more truthful as regards singular causal claims themselves, our causal skepticism or our common sense? According to our philosophical relativity hypothesis, neither position has an objectively determinate claim to be true or even to be the more truthful.

4. A Problem of Explanation

Although they have received their most extensive discussion in the philosophy of science, problems of explanation, like those of causation, are in fact quite general. Some question arises, whether in the course of a searching inquiry or a more casual conversation. Someone offers a sentence by way of explanation; he attempts to provide a certain sort of helpful answer to the question that arose. Did his offering constitute a genuine explanation of whatever it was that, presumably, his audience wanted explained?

Suppose that the question that arose was why certain pipes break when the water in them freezes. The sentence offered might then be this: 'The explanation of that is that when water freezes it expands'. In certain contexts, that will serve the people involved well enough in matters of understanding. How will that work?

By offering a simple sentence, the utterer gets the questioners to focus on some rather complex thought that relates the objective factual matters to their particular interests. A suitable thought often might be this: Among the facts bearing on the question of why those pipes then break, one that will fully serve relevant understanding of the matter is that water expands when it freezes. In the situation at hand, that thought might be true or correct. When the questioners take this attended thought as correct, as they may easily do, they are apt to feel well served and satisfied. They will take it that the offered sentence expressed a truth, that the speaker offered a genuine explanation.

The format just considered is meant to be quite general. Those seeking an explanation, or most responsible for getting the question to arise, need not be in any doubt as to the basic facts bearing on the breaking of the pipes. For example, they might just be testing the general knowledge, and the ability to use it, of the person prompted to offer the explanation sentence. So, *their* understanding of the matter will *not be increased* upon their acceptance of that offering, since they know too much already. Nonetheless, they may think that the offered sentence *articulates* relevant understanding of the matter itself; thus, they may be satisfied that, in that way, the fact that water expands when it freezes adequately serves relevant understanding of the matter in question. Within reasonable bounds, at any rate, our format for attended thoughts helps describe our propensities toward explanatory behavior.

While recognizing these trends in ordinary discourse, a philosopher may hold that such highly contextual considerations do not have much to do with genuine explanation. He will see explanations as some sort of ideal for which to strive but seldom if ever realized: When something actually *explains* something else, is a true *explanation* of it, then it fully and clearly *reveals* the other, perhaps as inevitably following from the (necessary) nature of the universe. Among actual philosophers, there is a spectrum of opinion on the matter, spanning the range from such a highly stringent characterization as this last, through requirements of intermediate stringency to some very liberal, highly contextual view of explanation.[10]

Are there genuine teleological explanations? If an extremely high standard must be met, then probably not; if only a contextual standard, then probably so. "Why do people take vacations?" someone asks. "In order to relax and enjoy themselves," someone else tries to explain. How well will this attempt serve understanding of the matter broached by the question? By some ideal invariant standard, seldom approached even in matters of familiar cause-and-effect operations, it is not served adequately; but, by the standard (more directly) involved in the conversation at hand, well enough we may suppose.

Without filling in the details, we may notice candidate explanations as possessing certain desirable features to a greater or lesser degree: how (nearly) complete they are, how readily intelligible, how clarifying and revealing, and others. A skeptic about explanation may claim that genuine explanations, not mere "explanation sketches," must have (certain of) these features in the highest degree or at least in a higher degree than is ordinarily exemplified. Candidates that have the features only in some lesser degree may serve various current purposes concerning understanding very well indeed. But that, a skeptic may reply, is just a pragmatic or psychological consideration. Since these objectively lesser candidates are (almost) all we ever offer, the skeptic concludes, we (almost) never *explain* anything.

For such a skepticism to prevail, there should be a semantics for relevant sentences, with 'explanation' and with 'explain', in which a high standard is always in force. The standard will not vary from context to context but will remain invariant. What will vary is how much various explanatory offerings each depart from this invariantly high standard and how much the contexts of those offerings allow for a departure then to be an acceptable one. With such an invariantist semantic approach in hand, skepticism about explanation will seem attractive. Without it, and with our focus on a contextual semantics for these sentences, the skepticism will seem all but unmotivated.

Is skepticism about explanation *correct,* though, or does truth lie with commonsense judgments about explanation? That depends on what semantics is most accurate for relevant sentences with 'explains'. If semantic relativity applies here, as it seems to do, then there is no determinate answer to this latter question. And, if that is so, then neither will there be an objective answer to the issue between this skepticism and the judgments about explanations that are endorsed by common sense. Perhaps we have here yet another instance of philosophical relativity.

It would be interesting, no doubt, to locate still further problem areas where philosophical relativity might obtain. But we shall forgo these somewhat particular inquiries now.

5. Categorical Problems and Conditional Problems

As we have considered them, three of our presented problems differ from the fourth. The problem of knowledge, the problem of causation and the problem of explanation are all *categorical* problems: If the skeptical side should be right in these issues, then the terms in question will fail to apply; we will fail to know and to explain things and will not have cited the causes of particular things. The problem of power and freedom, in contrast, is a hypothetical or, perhaps better, a *conditional* problem: The more skeptical side there is that of incompatibilism. What does this thesis say? It says nothing categorical; it does not say that so many things are not within our power or are not freely done by us. What it says, rather, is that, *if* determinism is true, then that is the consequence. The situation should be clear: Incompatibilism leaves it an open question whether or not determinism is true, that is, whether or not everything that happens is the inevitable outcome of prior considerations, a question it does not begin to address. The view leaves it open whether or not we have our presumed freedom and power.

The distinction between categorical and conditional marks, I believe, an important difference in philosophical problems. It is a difference that is important in understanding the attitudes toward these problems taken by contemporary philosophers.

As I said early in this discussion, philosophers are about evenly divided on our problem of power and freedom, a problem of determinism's consequences. About half are incompatibilists, and about half are compatibilists; at any rate, both sides are heavily represented. Now, incompatibilists are *at least moderately* skeptical in their view of this problem area. But are they any *more* skeptical than that, or are they also at most moderately skeptical? As we shall observe, the skepticism of (almost all) incompatibilists is only a moderate one.

One who is a skeptic on a categorical problem goes strongly against our commonsense view of things. Since most philosophers are very loath to do that, especially nowadays, few contemporary thinkers are skeptics on such problems. One who is a skeptic on a merely conditional problem, however, does not go against nearly so much of our commonsense view. Feeling much constrained by common sense, but perhaps not so much by very much else, many philosophers will be skeptics only on merely conditional problems.

The point is a general one. But it is particularly well illustrated, I think, by the attitudes of philosophers concerning the situation of our putative power and freedom. Some compatibilists believe determinism to be true, some believe it to be untrue, and some suspend judgment on the matter. There seems a roughly equal threefold division here. But, even while agreeing with most of common sense, a compatibilist can afford to take any of these stances on the question of determinism's truth: No matter which stance is taken, he will not thereby question the presumed fact, presumed by common sense, of our considerable freedom and power.

There is scarcely any division on the matter of determinism's truth, in contrast, among those who take the thesis to have strong implications. Almost every incompatibilist believes determinism itself to be untrue; they think that, while many occurrences may indeed be inevitable, plenty are *not* determined by prior considerations. Almost no incompatibilists believe determinism to be true, and, what is more, very few even suspend judgment on the matter. Among incompatibilists, only one of the three noted stances is at all heavily represented, a strikingly different story from the situation of the compatibilists.

The skepticism of almost all incompatibilist philosophers is, then, only a very moderate one; they do not depart much from the core of commonsense thinking. Rather, they only declare dire consequences to follow from a thesis they actually hold to be false, one whose implications are taken as merely hypothetical.

What sort of thinkers in this problem area take a stance that is roughly as skeptical (and so roughly as counterintuitive) as those taken by (categorical) skeptics concerning knowledge, explanation, and causation? The answer is, of course, simple: Those thinkers who hold *both* that determinism is true *and* that, if it is, the consequences are dire. Among all the positions in this deterministic neighborhood, this is the only one that holds, flat out, that we never do anything freely or of our own free will. Going very heavily against common sense indeed, this is also the only position in the neighborhood, as far as I can tell, that is taken by scarcely any (contemporary) philosophers.

This illustrates and helps to emphasize the point we raised about the great influence of common sense on philosophical attitudes. In the present context, this point should be borne in mind very clearly and firmly for two reasons. First, though the natures of the clashes are different, like traditional skepticisms, our relativity hypotheses also go against much of commonsense thinking. Therefore, we should not be surprised if most philosophers are, for the most part or in most moods, repelled by our present conjectures. Such a negative feeling, I would like to suggest, might be only a reflection of the fact, already acknowledged, that our theses are indeed uncommonsensical.

Second, just as antipathy to our hypotheses is itself apt to be determined by adherence to common sense, so such objections as philosophers might bring against the relativities are likely to arise from such adherence. If this is their source, then perhaps we may hope to see that, in the end, the main charges amount to nothing more than this: that our hypotheses are incompatible with certain of the more central beliefs of commonsense thought. Now, this incompatibility with common sense is, as must be admitted, a problem for our hypotheses. Nonetheless, if that is the greatest trouble for them, things will not be so bad for our relativistic conjectures. For, though this is a difficulty not to be taken lightly, it is scarcely overwhelming.

Now, most philosophers are, I think, prepared to agree with this assessment. That is why, as I believe, proponents of common sense, including the great majority of contemporary philosophers, would look to offer an objection that is more powerful and profound. But, if we examine the situation carefully, we might conclude that there is nothing more to say against our hypotheses than that they are, to a rather high degree, contrary to shared commonsense thinking.

IV

On the Status
of Ostensible Intuitions

We often respond to particular cases or examples, it is true, as though our ordinary terms semantically apply, both in what we say out loud and even in what we judge to ourselves. We do this both for actual cases, perceived as well as described, and for hypothetical examples, perforce only described and not perceived. Some of the hypothetical cases are very much like those encountered in the actual world. Others are quite unlike them, some even being wild and bizarre. Even through all of this departure from reality, nonetheless, we sense a continuity in our responses. Thus, philosophers postulate a continuity, too, a certain commonality, in whatever it is that is causally responsible for the occurrence of all of these responses. Now, *some* such postulation is, we may agree, almost certainly appropriate. Disagreement might occur, though, as regards the characterization of the underlying influence. We must ask, then, in an inquiring spirit, what *is* this common causal factor so widely efficacious on our (potential) behavior?

Philosophers have assumed without question that the dominant factor is our semantic understanding of the terms deemed appropriate or inappropriate to the correct description of the cases. Our elicited responses, which are often called our "intuitions," thus are assumed to reflect our semantic grasp of these terms and, only a bit less directly, to reflect the semantic conditions of the expressions themselves. Therefore, our responses to examples are the data to which an adequate semantic account of our common words must conform, if not with absolute strictness, then at least without very much leeway.

Now, it should be apparent that the semantic approach suggested in these pages is at odds with the one that is so widely assumed. Our suggestion, to the contrary, is that often there is only a very indirect connection, and an incomplete

65

one, between a hearer's (dominant) response to an example and (his understanding of) the semantics of a term the speaker then employs. This may be so, we suggest, whether the response is overt or covert; whether the example is actual, mildly hypothetical, or downright wild; whether the speaker and hearer are distinct or identical.

It might well be expected, then, that those who so unquestioningly assume the approach that is so prevalent will object vigorously to our relativistic proposals, in particular, to our hypothesis of semantic relativity. They will object in terms that derive from the semantic approach they adopt without question, offering what we may call *the objection from semantic intuitions*. The main aim of this chapter will be to examine, and then to begin to disarm, this objection to our hypothesized relativity.

1. The Objection from Semantic Intuitions

An objector may ask us to consider, for instance, a standard or paradigmatic case of the affirmative use of 'flat': Suppose that someone perceives a tabletop squarely before him, seeing the surface to be, as it is, less irregular, bumpy, and curved than (virtually) any tabletop he has ever seen. Suppose that conditions of communication, like those of perception, are straightforward enough, so the subject is as cooperative as can be. When asked about that tabletop, as regards its flatness, he responds by saying, "It is flat." His response appears quite sincere, and certainly is not insincere. What does his response indicate? Given the surrounding suppositions in force, the subject's response reflects his semantic understanding of 'flat'. Were his response covert rather than overt or made to a mere description of a case rather than to more direct stimulation, we would readily recognize his response to be an intuition. So begins the objection from semantic intuitions.

How does this objection conclude? At least in general outline, like this: An adequate account of 'flat' will have the word's semantics conform to such intuitions, and so an adequate account will be a contextualist one, since only a contextualist treatment will allow the word to apply semantically to the tabletop our subject perceives. An invariantist account, in contrast, will not have 'flat' be true of that tabletop, at least for the reason of some very tiny, perhaps microscopic, irregularities. An invariantist account will not conform to semantic intuition and, thus, must be rejected. Accordingly, there really is no semantic relativity here but only some complicated reasoning to such an erroneous effect. Good semantic methodology, one must agree, undermines this deceptive argumentation.

Much the same can be said for terms of more philosophical interest: Oftentimes, our intuitive responses with 'know' and 'free' and 'cause', responses to presumed ordinary situations, are markedly affirmative. Therefore, a correct semantics of these terms, structured to fit these affirmative reactions, will only be a contextualist one. These terms, just like 'flat', will often apply semantically. Not only is semantic relativity an illusion to be rejected, but with it we should reject as well the hypothesis of philosophical relativity.

In the current context, in which considerable relativistic argument has already been presented, this objection seems to beg the question against our relativity hypotheses: The objection amounts to a mere denial of these hypotheses rather than to an argument against them. For what does an alleged semantic intuition involve? To be both realistic and relevant to our topic, a respondent's ostensible intuition must involve at least this much: First, he must have a belief, or a belief-like state or attitude, that the tabletop is flat. And, second, that belief must be *true* or correct; otherwise, there will be no genuine intuition to which theory must conform. For there to be the wanted intuition, then, it must be determinately *true* that the perceived tabletop *is flat.* But, of course, whether or not this is so is precisely the issue we have been raising for some time now: Our relativistic argumentation has suggested that there is no determinate truth in any such matter. What is required to rebut these arguments is an argument to opposite effect, not any denial of their conclusion. The objection from semantic intuition, it appears, amounts only to such irrelevant denial.

Now, even if this objection does beg the question and does so as badly as I have suggested, the psychological force of the charge will still be great with many philosophers. For, as we have noted, many philosophers assume without question the semantic methodology from which this objection arises. Because they are so impressed with that prevalent approach, they will persist in thinking that somehow there must be some special force to this objection. Consequently, I will try to examine this objection as carefully as I can and even try to be charitable in its direction.

2. Semantic Intuitions Concerning Problematic Words

Before undertaking this examination, let me abort what would be an unfortunate impression: Even as an advocate of semantic relativity, I am not saying that we have *no* semantic intuitions whatever about 'flat' and fellows. Rather, the idea is that we have none that fully determine response. This idea merits, I think, some amplification.

To whatever extent they do have determinate semantic conditions, we have at least some understanding of the conditions of such terms as 'flat' and 'empty', not to exclude 'certain', 'know', 'free', 'power', 'cause', 'explain', and other philosophical favorites. This understanding is, no doubt, responsible for beliefs we have regarding these words, beliefs that are *partly* responsible for our responses to examples as well as for various more-detached responses. For instance, although we sense a semantic similarity between 'flat' and 'empty', we also sense a semantic difference: Both words purport to exclude, either absolutely or to a contextually indicated extent, certain items from other items. The word 'flat' purports to exclude such items as irregularity of shape, bumps or bumpiness, and curves or curvature from such items as surfaces, tops, and sides of material objects and areas of some such things (a field being, say, an area of the surface of the earth). The word 'empty', in contrast, purports to exclude such items as matter from such as space, or regions or volumes of space, to exclude such as the presumed contents of things from such as may contain them. The differences, like the similarities, are often reflected in response.

A man may face a cubical container. When someone points at what is before him and asks 'Is it *flat?*' the man will inspect the salient *side* relative to the pointing and judge *it* with regard to exclusion of shape irregularity, bumpiness, and the like. When the question is 'Is it empty?' the hearer will inspect, indirectly at least, the *inside* of the container and judge *it* with regard to exclusion of matter, perhaps liquid or gas. To be sure, his response will be determined as well by the stringency of the standards of exclusion he deems in force in the context. But which *sort* of standards those are, what is to be applied in respect to what excluded, is a prior consideration. The relevant prior considerations we manage, very well, to associate with the appropriate words. In large measure, this may be attributed to our semantic understanding of these words, which, along with other things, is reflected in various of our responses.

But how much semantic understanding do we have of these words; how much semantics is there to be understood? As much as just indicated and at least this much more: If in a given context, two comparable items are such that the first has notably *less* in the way of surface irregularity than does the second, then we will be disposed to withhold 'flat' from the second should we withhold it from the first. And similarly with 'empty'. What we have here is aimed at the real features of the things to be described, not at the appearances affected. This, too, is reflected in our responses to examples.

Suppose that we recently discovered the following widespread, systematic illusion: The things we have been calling flat are surrounded by a substance or a force field that gives them the appearance of having comparatively little surface irregularity. As well, the forces get these objects to meet our needs concerning so-called flat things: When they are horizontal, objects do not roll off them; little friction or resistance, however, is met when we try to slide objects across them, and so on. For all of this, when we break through the appearances, we find these force-infused items to have significantly more in the way of bumps and crevices than very many objects from which we have withheld 'flat'. We ask ourselves, with regard to this wildly hypothetical example, "If this should be, and should have been, the situation, will there be, and would there have been, flat items properly so-called by us or not?" My dominant response, presumably my semantic intuition, is in the negative: Whether or not there will have been *any* flat physical items at all, the ones we would have *called* flat will *not* have been flat objects.

Even if such terms as 'flat' and 'empty' are importantly indeterminate along certain dimensions of meaning so that they will not, in fact, semantically apply to any objects at all, this is not to say that they have *nothing* in the way of meaning or of semantic features. Apparently, they do have something, and rather a lot. Apparently, we understand these semantic features well enough, and this understanding *helps* to determine various of our responses with these terms. Semantic relativity, as well as invariantism, can allow all of this and may even welcome these facts. What relativity does not allow is this: That *everything* that passes for semantic intuitions with these words really does indicate semantic understanding on our part, that *everything* that helps to determine our responses with these words is a reflection of our understanding of conditions that they have. For semantic relativity, there is not enough in the way of determinate conditions for the understanding of meaning to play such a very large part in determining our responses to cases. In large measure, some other determinants must be operating as well.

3. The Objection Reformulated

According to the objection from semantic intuitions, this is not so. Our affirmative responses with 'flat' for good tabletops are wholly determined by our understanding of the fully determinate semantics of the word, which is a contextualist semantics. As I said, this objection seems to beg the question, and quite badly so, against the hypothesis of semantic relativity, for which conjecture systematic arguments have been given. But, as I also said, we will try to interpret the objection in such a way that it does not seem so obviously devoid of any special force.

One way of being charitable is to suppose this: The objector, who is a commonsense philosopher, is an implicit contextualist. He may make his contextualism explicit and challenge an invariantist to deal with the phenomenon of *ostensible* intuition. In particular, he may say the invariantist cannot even allow that the respondent *believes* that the tabletop is flat. Now, even if the invariantist denies that there is a *correct* belief here, denies that it is true that the surface is flat, he must admit, a reformulated objection runs, that the respondent does believe the tabletop to be flat. But it seems, finally, that such an admission is inconsistent with invariantism.

This reformulation can be put in simpler terms: Usually with no harm done, philosophers (myself included) swing between two senses for "intuitions." On the one hand, there is the meaning we have just been employing, in which correctness or truth is required for an intuition to be present; otherwise, it was just a misleading ostensible intuition. And, on the other hand, there is a sense in which there is no such requirement and in which at least a fair number of genuine intuitions can be misleading. We can advance our reformulation most simply by suggesting a switch from the first sense to the second. Perhaps we should then call it a reinterpretation rather than a reformulation, but no matter.

However expressed and however categorized, our intended reformulation wants more motivation: Why would it be thought, by a sophisticated objector, that an invariantist could not allow our respondent to have the belief that the tabletop *is flat?* Well, it appears that on the invariantist's account of 'is flat' the very meaning of the expression is this: *is such that nothing could ever be flatter.* And this seems to deprive invariantism of the chance to attribute the belief in flatness to our normal respondent. In the first place, if asked whether the latter, lengthy expression is true of the tabletop, the respondent would answer in the negative. And, in the second place, just as all theorists agree, the respondent *has* the belief that the tabletop is *not* such that nothing could ever be flatter. Could the respondent really have two beliefs that so *obviously* contradict each other? Could he, that is, have both the belief that this object is *not* such that nothing could be flatter *and* the belief that the object *is* such that nothing could be flatter? It seems unlikely. Therefore, there appear two reasons to suppose that, for invariantism, a belief in the tabletop's flatness is unattributable to a normal human subject, such as our respondent.

If this is indeed the case, then it seems that there is a new consideration here brought against the invariantist position and, with that, against the relativity hypotheses as well. Perhaps the objection from semantic intuitions, as reformulated or reinterpreted, does have some special force against our relativity hypotheses.

4. Two Invariantist Replies

As just reformulated, the objection challenges the invariantist to allow for the existence of a certain belief, for example, a respondent's belief that a perceived tabletop is *flat,* in situations in which such a belief does appear to be present. To this challenge, the invariantist must respond in either of two main ways: First, he may say that, despite appearances, there really is no such belief as that one present in the situation. Or, second, he may agree that there is that belief, on his account a false one, and say how it is consistent with his view that the belief be there. I suggest that both of these responses can be made at least somewhat plausible, though, of course, any given invariantist must eventually make a choice between them. Now, given our argumentation in the first three chapters, it is, of course, only to be expected that at least one of these main responses be at least moderately plausible. But let us see, in a bit of detail, the ways in which this expectation might be fulfilled.

The more "natural" line for the invariantist to take is, I suppose, the first of the two: to deny that the respondent actually believes that the tabletop *is flat*. Supposing it to be more natural, this was the position we supposed for our invariantist in chapter II, section 2, where these matters were first broached. How would an invariantist pursue this first main line?

The general strategy is clear enough. The invariantist will point to various other beliefs in the neighborhood that, on any plausible explanatory approach, the respondent will be reckoned to have. He will note how well (some of) these other beliefs can account for the subject's behavior. He will also note how easily the subject might confuse having (some of) these other beliefs with having the belief that the tabletop is flat. What beliefs will answer these explanatory interests?

In the first place, we should agree to this much: For him to engage in adaptive behavior in the area, it will be good for our respondent to have beliefs that not only pertain to the topic area but are *true*. But, on any even moderately appealing semantic approach, he may very well have plenty. For one thing, on all our approaches, he will believe that the tabletop is *sufficiently close*, for purposes most likely to be at hand, to being such that nothing could ever be flatter. For another, on all our approaches, he will believe that it is *not* the case that the tabletop is such that nothing could ever be flatter. And, on all our approaches, these beliefs, and more, may very well be true and correct. So, even if he lacks the belief that the tabletop is flat, the respondent will not lack for adequate guides to adaptive behavior in the area.

In the second place, our subject may have some false beliefs, or at least beliefs that are not true, so long as these do not much impair his behavioral adaptivity. Some such beliefs as these might explain his quick responses in verbal interchanges, in particular, his quick assent to a question such as "Is the tabletop flat?" To explain quick affirmative response, the invariantist can point to this belief, at the level of language: that the sentence, 'The tabletop is flat', as relating to the then-current circumstances, is true or expresses a truth. And the respondent, it can be added, will believe the same thing about many relevantly similar sentences in relation to relevantly similar circumstances. Now, on any plausible account, the belief about the sentence in question is distinct from, even if closely related to, the alleged belief that the tabletop is flat. At the same time, the two beliefs, or candidate beliefs, may be readily and systematically confused in almost all conversational situations. Now, although the language-level belief must be admitted to obtain by any account, the object-level candidate can be denied the status of genuine belief. Because the two are so readily confused and because we do have the language-level belief, we quickly and unreflectively respond as though we have the object-level belief, also. At least in outline, that explains our affirmative linguistic behavior.

For the invariantist, this first line of reply can be pursued a good deal further and, I think, developed with considerable plausibility. But let us now turn, instead, to discuss the second main line of reply that might be available to him.

Along this other main line, the invariantist will contend that he can allow the respondent to believe not only the various propositions lately noted and further ones of a similar stripe but even, simply, that the tabletop is flat. There are at least three ways for him to attempt this plausibly, each contesting the contextualist's challenging argument in a different place or way. To see the invariantist's alternatives, let us remind ourselves of that challenging argument and even amplify it to some degree.

First, it is argued that, on the invariantist account, 'is flat' means the same as 'is such that nothing could ever be flatter'. Now, *second,* on the standard Fregean view of the matter, accepted by many philosophers, when one synonymous expression is substituted for another in a nonquotational sentence that is true, the resulting sentence will have the same truth-value as the original. So, if we have as true 'The respondent believes the tabletop *is flat*', we will also have as true 'The respondent believes the tabletop *is such that nothing could ever be flatter*'. But this latter cannot be, the objector concludes: As we have agreed, the respondent believes the tabletop is *not* such that nothing could ever be flatter. And, *third,* a (normal) person cannot have two beliefs that so clearly and obviously contradict each other.

The objector's attack can be met in any of the three places indicated: First of all, the invariantist can say that though 'is such that nothing could ever be flatter' specifies an application condition of 'is flat', perhaps even the only application condition, the two need not mean exactly the same thing. The expression 'is a closed plane figure with three sides' specifies a condition, perhaps the only one, for the expression 'is a triangle', for the most central, standard meaning of both expressions. Yet, the meaning of each expression seems different from that of the other. Perhaps this actually is so. And perhaps, as well, much the same thing happens with the pair of expressions on which we are focusing. If so, then the Fregean line is quite irrelevant to the present issues, and the objection from intuitions, even as charitably reformulated, stops almost before it gets started.

Second, if we grant the objector his (dubious) claim of required synonymy, then the Fregean precept can be challenged. Concerning sentences attributing propositional attitudes, notably beliefs, this has been done by Benson Mates and, more recently, by Tyler Burge, quite well, in my opinion.[1] Burge's arguments in particular are somewhat intricate, too much so for me here to recapitulate them. But they are rather persuasive pieces of reasoning, as the reader may verify. Suppose, then, what is not implausible, that Mates and Burge, not the Fregeans, are correct in the matter. Then, the invariantist may (generously) grant that, on his semantics, 'is flat' must mean the same as 'is such that nothing could ever be flatter', but, nevertheless, he may still hold to a difference in truth-value for the corresponding belief sentences: Although he assigns truth to 'The respondent believes the tabletop is flat', he witholds it from the lengthier belief sentence. Once again, the invariantist need not attribute to the respondent the belief that the tabletop is such that nothing could ever be flatter.[2]

Third, even if he grants both of the foregoing assumptions to the objector, which may well be generosity to a fault, the invariantist can still reply with effect. This time he can make a point about the identity, or individuation, of beliefs. Suppose, then, that the respondent believes the tabletop is flat and, because he does, he believes the tabletop is such that nothing could ever be flatter. There might well be two beliefs here, running in perfect logical parallel, not just one belief twice described. The belief that the tabletop is flat will be causally quite operative. Its long-winded counterpart will be not only very inoperative but even generally inaccessible. Moreover, like the belief that it is flat, the belief that the tabletop is *not* such that nothing could ever be flatter can be reckoned causally efficacious to a considerable degree. As long as these differences of causal efficacy, and causal role, do obtain, as seems rather plausible, there will be no harm in attributing to people beliefs that are obvious contradictories of each other.

A difficult problem would arise, the invariantist might say, only when there are attributed two beliefs that not only are obvious contradictories but are efficacious for behavior to the same extent and, moreover, in the same contexts and ways. But, as we have seen, there are at least three ways, each somewhat plausible, of avoiding such a problem when there is attributed to a subject the (false) belief that a tabletop is flat.

We all agree, anyway, that we have plenty of beliefs that contradict plenty of others. And some philosophers have argued that such conflicts, often blatant ones, can be found at almost every psychological turn.[3] In attributing attitudinal inconsistencies, the invariantist will not be doing anything very novel. Rather, for the admittedly jumbled mentality we all do seem to have, he is just suggesting more of the same, and perhaps not very much more at that.

Along the second main line of reply, the invariantist can defend his position in any of a number of ways and with considerable plausibility. He can also do well enough here in a more positive direction to complement his chosen defense. Rather briefly, he can say this: The false belief that the tabletop is flat is, though false and not true, a useful belief for us to have. It gets us (more readily) to say such handy sentences as 'That's flat' when talking of surfaces in our environment. It gets us to accept such utterances from others. Not only do we talk with language, we also think in it. Without complex circumlocutions, both our conversations and our inferences proceed more rapidly and smoothly. For almost any common context, we are then better equipped to elicit, and to emit, adaptive behavior. Of course, there are the rare contexts in which the main interest is in semantic theory and philosophy. Then, but only then, we will want to recognize our false beliefs, however useful, for the erroneous attitudes that they are. But, with an invariantist theory brought to mind, we may do so whenever the need arises.

5. A Direct Relativist Reply

An invariantist reply to contextualism, and in particular to the objection from semantic intuitions, is also a reply for the relativist. For, when the first two positions are at an impasse or a standoff, a situation that seems so often to obtain, the relativity advocate has just what he wants. We might say, then, that we have just considered two lines of *direct* reply for the invariantist that are also *indirect* lines of reply for the relativist. Together, we may say further, these two lines constitute an indirect *avenue* of reply for the advocate of relativity.

I would like now to consider what I take to be a second avenue of reply for the relativity advocate. Not available to the invariantist, this is a *direct way for the relativist* to answer the objection from semantic intuitions. Along this second, direct avenue of reply, the relativist challenges, in a novel way, the objector's contention that we and our respondent do believe that tabletops are flat. Since there is a parallel here with the invariantist's second line, in taking this avenue the relativist will repeat some, but not all, of the things previously said by the invariantist in connection with this general matter.

The relativist will begin his reply, it is evident, with some novel and distinctively relativistic argumentation: Just as 'flat' itself has no (fully) determinate semantics, so we find indeterminacy in so many sentences in which the word essentially occurs (whether or not in all of them). In particular, there might well be no determinate semantics for 'He believes that the tabletop is flat', even as uttered of our respondent. If this is so, as is plausible enough, then it is not (determinately) true that the respondent believes that surface to be flat. Much of what has passed as the respondent's intuition thus appears to evaporate.

When the relativist takes this preemptive line, then, like the invariantist before him, he must be quick to note other beliefs for our respondent to have. Otherwise, he will be at a loss to explain the person's responsive behavior to an example and a related leading question. But such a belief is not far to find. The respondent believes that the sentence 'The tabletop is flat', as well as relevantly similar sentences, does express a truth. The belief that such a sentence expresses a truth and that it expresses a proposition relevant to the case and question encountered is, along with the usual attitudes also present, enough for forceful positive response at the verbal level. This is the only level at which such response is patent; perhaps it is the only level at which a genuine response is present at all when such terms as 'flat' are those most directly involved.

According to relativity, of course, the belief that such a sentence expresses a truth, a belief about a bit of language, is false, or at least not (determinately) true. Since it is less than (fully) determinate, the uttered sentence expresses no (classically) truth-valued proposition at all, let alone a proposition that is true. Nonetheless, the relativist can observe, this false belief about language may be a useful one for us to have: Our having it gets us more readily to utter and accept short, familiar, handy sentences so that our thinking can run quickly and smoothly toward flexible behaviors.

We can now enter the homestretch of this route of reply: To say that we have *semantic intuitions* about cases of everyday objects called 'flat' implies that, to such examples, people respond on the basis of, among other things, their *belief* that the item is *flat*. But relativity can deny that (it is determinately true that) we have just such a belief. So, on the hypothesis of semantic relativity, we question whether there really are semantic intuitions here. To assume that there are and to use that assumption to argue for the rejection of semantic relativity is, once again and after all, to beg the question against the semantic hypothesis we are trying to examine carefully and comprehensively.

6. How Commonsense Beliefs Account for Appearances of Intuitions: An Explanatory Sketch

So far we have presented various alternatives, all somewhat plausible, to the situation required by a forceful and relevant objection from semantic intuitions. Indeed, we have done quite a bit of that already, having outlined two main avenues of relativistic response, one direct and the other indirect, with the latter itself consisting of two main lines. But we have done comparatively little in the way of providing a positive explanation of how it might be that one or another of these alternatives is the situation that does obtain rather than the situation that our contextualist objection requires. As an addition to the material of our first three chapters, we have done relatively little in the way of providing a positive argument for thinking that the actual situation is one of these alternatives rather than as prevalently assumed.

In this section, I shall present the beginnings, quite sketchily, of such an additional more positive explanation and argument. In the chapter that follows, we shall delve more deeply into the material now to be outlined. This material should be regarded, I believe, as a third avenue of reply to the objection from semantic intuitions, both more aggressive than, but also complementary to, the two avenues we have been considering.

Now, in any case whatever, what a person's apparent intuitions most directly reflect are certain of his own attitudes, perhaps most notably certain of his strong implicit beliefs. For it is his attitudes themselves, of course, that are most directly productive of his own spontaneous responses, such responses as we often favor by calling them "intuitions." When people's intuitions about examples go together, as in the cases of flatness attribution just considered, we can infer that they have similar attitudes that similarly appear to them as relevant to the example's correct description. Pooling the responses of many to many examples, we can infer, somewhat less directly, an attitudinal system to which our society's members subscribe, the subscription being substantial, not complete, in the case of each individual. (More precisely, we may infer an at least moderately available part of such a system.) Now, any information we can hope to get from any of this as to any larger, less subjective matters, including the semantic conditions of our linguistic expressions, is, when obtainable at all, by way of inferences that are considerably more indirect.

When the inferences we make are quite indirect, there is room for our apparent data to lead us to conclusions we need not accept. This may happen with quite a few semantic matters, which are, after all, questions of how best to account for certain patterns of social behavior. In such cases, an appearance as to a semantic intuition may easily mislead us about the semantic conditions of common expressions.

Let us think again about our respondent uttering "It is flat," with some "feeling of correctness," in regard to the rather regular tabletop. Even if he does not actually believe that the tabletop is *flat,* as we have relativistically hypothesized, nonetheless he may believe that *the words he is uttering express a truth* (whatever the exact content of that truth in fact may be). And he may believe this very, very strongly. If he has such a strong belief, that may account for his feeling of correctness, for what is presumed to be or to indicate a semantic intuition as to the contextualist conditions of 'flat'. How would he come to have such a strong belief here, stronger than any belief he has as to *what* is the whole situation of the conditions of his 'flat'?

For almost any of our very ordinary words that we take as true of real things, such as 'cat' and 'dog', 'table' and 'chair', 'red' and 'blue', 'flat' and 'bumpy', and so on, we very, very strongly believe, I suggest, that there have been many things of the indicated "kinds." Supposing we have determinate beliefs about things of these kinds, we very, very strongly believe that there have been many cats and many dogs, many things red and many blue, many things bumpy, and many things flat. Moreover, I hypothesize, we believe very nearly as strongly that each of these words is true of each of the respectively suggested things: that 'cat' is true of many cats that have existed, that 'red' is true of many actual red things, that 'flat' is true of many things that have been flat. And, almost as strongly as that, I suggest, do we believe that many of *us* have *correctly* applied each of these words to certain of the things of which they are true: that many people in our society have correctly applied 'cat' to many entities that there have been, that many of us have correctly applied 'flat' to many objects that have been encountered. Even this last, I hypothesize, we believe more firmly than we do *almost* anything as to the putative properties (or relations) of the objects in question. For example, we may believe more strongly that we have correctly applied 'cat' to some encountered objects than we believe that (if there are cats, then) cats are animals. Along with this, we believe so strongly as well that, *providing* the objects we encounter do not much change in any relevant way and *providing* our linguistic habits do not change much, we will *continue to apply* these words *correctly* to objects encountered. Such beliefs in the *correct application* of our most ordinary individual "predicate" words pertain to objects, to people, and to situations. Although rooted in the past, with the noted provisos, the beliefs will pertain as well to the present and even to the future. Widely pervasive, these beliefs are, I conjecture, a very strong and central part of our commonsense thinking.

To take the case at hand, we all believe very strongly that we each have correctly applied 'flat' to many encountered objects taken to be fit for application of that common word. Moreover, we strongly believe that, *given* the example specified and *given* a constancy in our own descriptive tendencies, both assumed, we will apply 'flat' correctly with respect to our considered example. In particular, our chosen respondent, assumed to be a normal one among us, will do so.

It is just such beliefs concerning 'flat' that underlie the feeling of correctness in our respondent, and in ourselves, to the case of the good tabletop. Along with this strong belief, of course, other believed propositions figure in the reasoning issuing in his response, and in his feeling: (a) If *this* case, as given in the example's description, is *not* a case of something flat, then it is doubtful that so many of us have correctly applied 'flat' to any objects, cases, or situations at all or to more than hardly any. But (b) that cannot be. So, (c) this must be a case in which the term does apply.

The conditional proposition (a) is believed very strongly. This strength is *not* due to the respondent's thinking that good tabletops are just about the flattest things anywhere in physical reality; indeed, he probably does not think such an extreme thing at all. Rather, the supporting thoughts run along these lines: Whatever, if anything, is somehow preventing the proper application of 'flat' to such a "paradigmatic" tabletop situation must be a factor that cuts a very wide and deep path in such a negative direction: If things involved with this tabletop will not block this negative factor, then what will? Some rather less bumpy physical situation that, nonetheless, still falls short of the logically absolute limit? Perhaps so, but, on the other hand, who can be so sure? However dimly, a threat is sensed. But the threat to our beliefs in correct application *must* be blocked *somewhere*. So, seeing no inherently better place to take a stand, we had best take it right here and now with the good tabletop. Consequently, regarding this surface, one will respond with 'It is flat' and *feel* that one's response *must be correct*.

Moved by commonsense beliefs that are as unexciting as they are powerful, we may respond to examples without manifesting all that much in the way of semantic understanding. Even if we feel that this cannot be so and have strong feelings that we are *correctly* applying the word in question, it may well be so for all that. The prevalent approach to examples, giving rise to the objection from semantic intuitions, will not allow for such a possibility. But with the explanatory sketch just presented, we gain a glimpse of an alternative approach, more broadly psychological, that may prove at least as viable, and perhaps more so.

If our ostensible intuitions rather frequently mislead us about semantics, as now seems quite possible, then the most likely cases for such misleading will include those in which the expressions in question have no determinate semantics. For, in any such case, a response that seems to indicate a definite semantics that is such and such will not actually lead one against some semantic condition to the contrary. It will just have one favoring some one particular semantic line in a matter that is actually undecided and open, between that line and at least one other. Not much doubt about semantic intuitions need be generated, therefore, in order that the charge against our relativity hypotheses be effectively disarmed.

What we shall now argue, however, is that a great deal of this doubt is actually warranted. Even in linguistic matters in which, as far as we can tell, the expressions have some relevantly determinate semantic conditions, our responses often will seem to point to conditions that are unlikely candidates for those terms. That is because, we can hypothesize, even these responses are determined, at least in large part, by commonsense beliefs mute as to any specific semantic information. On this hypothesis, these common attitudes are as strong causally as they are silent semantically.

V

Two Approaches
to Ostensible Intuitions

Let us examine more closely the two approaches to our ostensible intuitions, to our cognitive responses, briefly touched on in the preceding chapter: first, the *prevalent approach*, as I call it, which takes spontaneous reactions to examples as almost always indicative of semantic conditions and, second, what I call the *broadly psychological approach*, which does not. To build a case for his semantic treatment, the invariantist must, I think, argue that the second of these approaches is objectively superior to the former. On the other hand, even if one is inclined to think the psychological approach superior, one need not be an invariantist. For a conspicuous illustration, one may just as well advocate the hypothesis of semantic relativity.

Now, our own position is, of course, that of relativity, not invariantism. And, it must be noted, to advocate a case for semantic relativity, one *need not* argue that the broadly psychological approach is superior. Rather, to rebut the objection from semantic intuitions, it is enough to argue that the psychological approach is *not inferior* to the more popular treatment. Nonetheless, throughout most of this chapter, I will be arguing that the psychological approach is indeed a superior way to account for (many of) our cognitive responses. I will do this for two main reasons: First, I am inclined to think that this stronger proposition may very well be correct. Second, by arguing in this way, I provide an *a fortiori* case for relativity against the objection from semantic intuitions. If we come to think that the provided case is not quite as strong as all that, we will have a fall-back schema already developed for maintaining the weaker proposition.

The chapter will be organized around the idea of undermining a certain theory of the semantics of many ordinary words, a view by now widely popular, that I call the *causal theory of (semantic) reference (for words)*. One reason for

79

this is that this theory, or its wide acceptance, is very largely motivated by the prevalent approach to responses to examples. Thinking about examples troublesome for the theory might, then, provide abundant concrete material for questioning its motivating methodology.

A second reason is that the sort of semantics outlined by the causal theory does not fit well with the hypothesis of semantic relativity. Of course, one can always claim that the causal theory will, at most, only apply to *certain* expressions while the relativity hypothesis will only apply to certain *other* expressions. Then, there would be no direct clash between the two. And this claim is, in my judgment, a very plausible one. But, for an advocate of relativity, it would be good to have, in addition, something stronger to say.

A third reason for this organization is that the causal theory has considerable interest for many philosophers, including many who may as yet have little interest in the ideas I am now advocating. By drawing on that already-extensive interest, I might move some to reconsider actively certain assumptions that would otherwise remain unquestioned by them, assumptions central to the prevalent approach.

Because of the organization I have chosen, this chapter is somewhat lengthy, and at times it moves away from the main themes of the essay as a whole. But such movements are, eventually, counterbalanced by movements of return. And the three reasons just cited, along with some others yet to emerge, do justify, I believe, any temporary digressions from our main course.

1. The Prevalent Approach to Responses and the Causal Theory of Reference

In one of his early papers, "It Ain't Necessarily So," Hilary Putnam introduced into the literature an example that has become highly influential in the philosophy of language, which I will call *the case of unlimited robotry for putative cats.*[1] According to this example, the things we humans have taken to be cats, in the most common meaning of that term, have always been inanimate robots unlike the things we have taken to be mice and dogs and tigers. The first group of robots was put down on earth many years ago, before the advent of human language, by scientists from Mars. Each Martian robot had an extremely tiny receiver in its "head," through which it constantly received signals sent by the Martians. These signals caused the "fleshy" robots to behave in the customary feline ways, even to "reproduce," so that the scenario would appear naturally ongoing. Were signals to cease impinging on any of the specimens, the robot would limply flop over, like a rag doll. But that just did not happen. Now, due to some modern investigatory techniques, it is only just recently, we may assume, that we have first become aware of any of this business and, also, of all of it.

To elicit response, one may ask of this case an appropriately leading question: "If this should be the actual situation, will there be, and will there have been, cats or not?" Even taking the question in its most common meaning, so that uncontested lions and tigers do not count, (in most contexts[2]) my *dominant* response, like Putnam's, is affirmative: There will still have been cats (they just will not have been animals). At the same time, I sense, as Putnam also seemed to do, a *dominated* response in the other direction.[3] My intuitions are in conflict, a conflict in which the affirmative response prevails. How is one to explain this pattern of response to the example?

On the prevalent approach, that favored by contemporary philosophical practice, we are to say that the responses show something about the semantics of 'cat'. The assumption is that our understanding of 'cat', of its semantic conditions, generates (our strongest belief, or beliefs, relevant to responding and, hence) our dominant response to the example. The dominated response, it is assumed, may be discounted or ignored. A semantic account of the word must then be sought that articulates this understood and productive condition. Giving this semantic account, which differs from any in which a condition of 'cat' is *animal,* fleshes out this sort of explanation. That meat was later provided, both by Putnam himself and by Saul Kripke, and has become widely known as *the causal theory of (semantic) reference (for words).*[4] On the prevalent methodological approach, therefore, we are to choose our semantic analyses so that our responses to examples conform to them. I shall be arguing that this prevalent approach, when followed consistently, leads us down a path of increasing dubiety. As a theory for words, the causal theory of reference is just an early step down this doubtful path.

What does the causal theory say about such words as 'cat'? Even though it is fairly sketchy, the following passage from Kripke's *Naming and Necessity* presents the leading points of the theory clearly enough for profitable reflection.

> For species, as for proper names, the way the reference of a term is fixed should not be regarded as a synonym for the term. In the case of proper names, the reference can be fixed in various ways. In an initial baptism it is typically fixed by an ostension or a description. Otherwise, the reference is usually determined by a chain, passing the name from link to link. The same observations hold for such a general term as 'gold'. If we imagine a hypothetical (admittedly somewhat artificial) baptism of the substance, we must imagine it picked out as by some such 'definition' as, 'Gold is the substance instantiated by the items over there, or at any rate, by almost all of them'. . . . I believe that in general, terms for natural kinds (e.g., animal, vegetable and chemical kinds) get their reference fixed in this way; the substance is defined as the kind instantiated by (almost all of) a given sample.[5]

First, the idea that favored single words should be treated in parallel with proper names is clear enough here. So is the more specific idea that it is the names that are to have pride of place, their treatment serving as the model for the other. With the talk of "a chain" and of "passing the name from link to link," it is reasonably clear that this model is a causal one.

On the causal theory, the paradigm of how a name has a bearer is this causal or quasi-causal model: In some initial acts, some people attach the name to an (intended) bearer. They do this by being, along with the bearer, involved in an appropriate network of causal or quasi-causal relations. Then, the name, as a name of that object, may be passed from these folks to others, all relevant parties being involved in an appropriate network of relations. These processes of passage can involve many people over much space and time. Finally, one of us now may use that name with a certain intention and, almost willy-nilly, our use involves reference to that bearer. The current user needs no special knowledge of the bearer but need only be appropriately involved in the network of relations with it, appropriate aspects of the network then being productive of that use of the name. Of course, this is a very crude statement of this view about names. Even so, it should be clear enough that this account of proper names is at least a plausible one.[6]

When we consider words, not proper names, the question of a bearer does not arise. But, as the quotation from Kripke suggests, the theory locates a sample of objects, or of stuff, in the place that the bearer had before. Then, something like baptismal acts are performed by certain people with regard to a favored word, say, 'gold' or 'cat', and to so many sample items that share some common nature or essence. This involves having those items in an appropriate causal or quasi-causal network along with the baptizers. For example, the people might be so many ancient Greeks who, through appropriate causal processes, are perceiving so much gold or so many cats and are coining the original cognate of our 'gold' or of our 'cat'. Then, by way of causal processes involved in communication, those Greeks pass the word along to other people, of later generations, who are involved with them in an appropriate network. Finally, I may receive the word or, more likely, an English equivalent. So, what my 'cat' is true of will be just those objects that are instances of the (salient) kind, the kind for the relevant essence, which was predominantly instanced in the sample for those crucially placed in the causal network reaching to me now. Presumably, as it happens, in the case of my 'cat', those objects were (a certain sort of) feline animal. But, from this theory's viewpoint, that is quite a secondary matter: Historical happenstance aside, the accepted semantic conditions on 'cat' may have the word be true of just some vegetables or else some robots, not animals at all.

To be fair to the causal theory, we can distinguish two versions of that account of words. Kripke, as we have noticed, presents a version that is highly historical in orientation. Except for subsequent semantic shifts, *not* to be invoked lightly, the reference of our terms was long ago fixed beyond flexible change. In the case of proper names, this relative inflexibility perhaps is no serious drawback. But with words it is very implausible. What our words are true of should not be so rigidly bound to what ancients encountered in their environment, perhaps objects quite unlike any we have ever faced. To lessen the initial implausibility of a causal theory of words, then, we should opt for a version of the theory that is less resolutely historical, that gives more weight to recently encountered objects. At times, Putnam advocates such a more current version.[7] This version decreases the similarity in treatment for words and for names. That makes it less implausible. But, since there is still a lot of similarity of treatment left while the two sorts of expressions themselves seem so different semantically, this only lessens the implausibility of the theory for words; it does not remove it.[8]

The apparent implausibility of the view did not deter its advocates from propounding it vigorously and at length. What led them to do this was, in largest measure, the view's apparent ability to explain our responses to certain examples, reactions that seem, at least on the prevalent approach, otherwise inexplicable. So, at base their motivation was, in large part, a reliance on this popular method. Now, given this approach, the theory seems to explain our response to Putnam's case of unlimited robotry, to take a most conspicuous instance: In that case, the essence of the objects encountered in connection with "baptizing" uses of 'cat' is, presumably, to be a certain sort of robot. So, the word will project to, and be true of, just such other objects as have that same essence. Among those objects will be, most notably, entities later encountered and called cats by us. All these objects will fall in the extension of the word; all of them will be cats, which is our dominant response to the example.

The prevalent approach requires an explanation in terms of semantic understanding. For a sufficiently clever and troubling example, like Putnam's influential case, the understanding imputed will be of conditions specified by an initially implausible theory.

2. Some Problems for the Causal Theory and for the Prevalent Approach

As one may observe, there is a problem for the causal theory as regards finding some limit to the common words for which it applies: Although the theory is moderately, though only very moderately, credible as an account of such words as 'cat' and 'gold', it would seem less plausible even than that as an account of such words as 'pencil', 'pediatrician', and 'bachelor'. At the same time, and unfortunately for the theory, examples that (at first) appear to support the idea that the theory works for the first words are paralleled by examples that would seem to support, even if not *quite* as strongly, the idea that the theory works for the second group as well.[9] But the main problems for the causal theory of words arise in connection with various further examples, readily concocted, involving even those words, like 'cat', for which the view was originally intended. With each of these examples, the dominant responses of most people go in one direction, while, given the prevalent approach to examples, the predictions of the theory go otherwise. If one continues to accept the prevalent methodology, it will be noted, these initial responses will directly undermine the causal theory for words. Moreover, one will then seek to articulate a very much more complicated semantics for 'cat' and company, the implicit understanding of which generated the unpredicted responses. Will this complex semantics be offset by a compensating simplicity somewhere in the account of our responses? Perhaps so, but it is far from obvious that it will. Thus, our response patterns might be indicating little about semantic matters and more about certain other things. What other things? Certain of our attitudes, of course. Which ones? Let us defer an attempt to answer until we have an instructive variety of responses elicited and observed.

A. Examples with Disparate Pasts and Futures

According to this theory, as long as the causal network is in place, suitably linking us with enough sample items with a common nature or essence, the word used for, fixed to, those items will apply to further entities with that same nature, and not to objects with quite a disparate nature, not represented in the sample. So far as semantics goes, there is *no further importance in the specific natures of any of the objects in question*: If 'cat' was fixed to only some vegetables, then only such vegetables will be objects of which the word is true; if it was fixed to only some animals, then only such animals will be in the extension, and so on. Do our responses accord with this theoretical pronouncement? To some extent, of course, they do; otherwise, the causal theory would never have been propounded. But to a considerable extent they do not.

Here is an example that, I think, shows this quite clearly, a *case of feline robots in the past and feline animals in the future*. This example involves a change in the population of specimens that, in conjunction with uses of 'cat', we humans encounter over time. The moment of the change will be assumed to be the present time, right now: Up until now, this example is just like Putnam's classic case, with Martian robots as the objects of our uses of 'cat'. At the present time, the Martians are, in an undetected flash, replacing each robot with a similar appearing "duplicate" animal. From here on out, we will be using 'cat' in encounters with such animals, there being no robots any longer on our planet.

Now, since this case will involve *one's own* thought and behavior from here on out, it will help if we explicitly assume that we all are to be ignorant of *any* of these presumed discrepancies from the actual situation. We are to think of ourselves *as believing* all along that we have been encountering only such feline animals and that we will continue to do so. In other words, our beliefs in the example are relevantly the same as those we now actually do have.

Where did the Martians get the animals to put in place of the most recent robots? We may assume what we like (for most subjects, it will not matter much in eliciting responses). So, for one, the Martians could have synthesized the animals, in a cell-by-cell manner, perhaps getting them to be "enough like" and "enough different from" pumas and tigers they had observed. Alternatively, the Martians could have captured some pumas many thousands of years ago and, by inducing and selecting appropriate mutations, could have bred them down to obtain the current generation of small tame creatures. With an eye to the impending replacement, they could have engineered the convergence in appearance of their animal breed and their robots.

In such a situation, what entities, if any, will be cats? Without undue theorizing, my dominant response is that *both* the past robots *and* the future animals will be cats. Given customary methodology, my dominant response is contrary to the prediction of the causal theory: The theory would have my response be that the future animals are *not* cats. For no feline animals were in the sample faced by us human speakers.

Although that is my own response here, and it seems to be the most typical one, there is another dominant reaction that is also rather typical for theoretically uncommitted subjects: that only the future animals are cats, not the past robots. Given the accepted approach to examples, this response goes even more strongly against the causal theory. This is so because with this second typical reaction, the theory disagrees not only in regard to the future animals but in regard to the past robots as well.

There is a common aspect to them that means trouble for the causal theory. At the same time, we have noticed *individual differences* of dominant response to our considered example. This matter of individual differences is, I think, a most severe problem for the customary methodology. On that approach, there is always some single correct sort of response, which is philosophically revealing. For any who do not make this response dominantly, some special psychological factor must be invoked, and one that is to the discredit of the respondents: They are confused in such and such a way; their intuitions are not sufficiently sensitive; or whatever. But I do not think that, in response to interesting examples, there must always be a right answer, with other typical responses then being somehow wrong. On the contrary, each of several responses may be quite typical, each for a different group of normal, intelligent respondents, with no group being philosophically credited at the expense of any other.[10]

This complex psychological matter of individual differences is a recurrent theme to be observed with many examples. It always means trouble for the customary methodology. Having mentioned the generality now, I will not bother to make many particular references.

The difficulty for (almost) any semantic theory to explain much with *cases with disparate pasts and futures* is highlighted when we consider, in conjunction with the case already before us, the *inverse* of that example: a *case of feline animals in the past and feline robots in the future*. In this inverse example, there have been many feline animals around right up until now; in relevant respects, the world up until now is just as we actually believe it to have been. Right now, the Martians replace each such animal with a "duplicate" robot in an undetected flash. In presumed suitable ignorance, we will be encountering henceforth only such feline robots. (What do the Martians do with the replaced animals? Well, they can destroy all of the beasts, cruel as that is.)

What is our dominant response to this situation? Typically, it is that the past *animals are* cats but the future *robots* are *not*. (Also typically, I notice no conflicting dominated responses here.) This contrasts interestingly with our responses to the just previous case, itself the inverse of this present example.

With these two examples, we have a relevantly symmetric, or parallel, pair of cases. But our most typical responses to these examples are importantly divergent. What are we to make of this discrepancy? For one thing, it indicates that, for our cognitive responses, the specific assumed natures of the objects involved really do make a difference, not as the causal theory would have it. When it is certain mammalian animals in the future, then, even when only unlike objects are encountered in the past, we are ready to reckon the future items cats. When it is robots, in contrast, we will not count the future items cats of any sort. Do we want an (internalized) *semantic* theory, rather than a more broadly psychological view, to explain our divergent responses here? Perhaps, but the prospect does not seem an especially inviting one.

B. Three Related Types of Examples:
Epistemological, Metaphysical, and Combined

In discussing the status of such statements as 'cats are animals', Kripke adduces two main types of examples. Although interestingly related, the examples of the two types are quite different, as Kripke emphasizes.

In the first sort of example, which we may call *epistemological,* we suppose that, all along, we have been *wrong* about the "sort of thing" we have been encountering. It is examples of this type on which we have been focusing so far. So, in particular, Putnam's case of unlimited robotry for putative cats is a case of this epistemological type: In that case, we have been wrong about what general sort of thing putative cats are; we have taken them to have been animals when, all along, they have been robots and not animals.

In the second type of example, we have been *right,* not wrong, about the general sort of encountered things. What we do this time is to suppose that, *instead* of things of this sort, there *were* at the same places and times, and giving off the same appearances, things of *another* general sort. Let us call examples of this second type *metaphysical*. Correlative with Putnam's epistemological example, we may contemplate this metaphysical case: Suppose that, in all the places where the relevant feline animals are and have been, there were instead just so many feline robots. Then, we have the question of describing that situation: *Would* those robots be, and have been, cats or not?[11]

As Kripke points out, we have *different dominant responses,* or different intuitions, in trying to describe the two sorts of examples: For the epistemological case, when we ask the question "*Will* there have been cats anyhow?" our dominant response is yes. For the metaphysical case, when we ask the parallel question "*Would* there have been cats anyhow?" our dominant response is no. This discrepancy in response came as a surprise to many philosophers, who must have assumed implicitly that our responses with regard to such related examples should be the same. Kripke's noted discrepancy raised a question for explanation: Why do we make different responses to the two sorts of cases? The causal theory of reference offers an answer to this question. And it seems often thought that a main strength of this theory lies in its ability to give an adequate answer.

Here is another example, a combination of the two just considered. Let us call cases of this third type *combined* examples. For this present combined example, we *begin* by supposing that we have gotten things badly *wrong* about putative cats; the items have all been robots and not animals. That is the epistemological part. We want to combine a metaphysical part with it. So, *given* that surprising actuality, we are to contemplate the following "doubly" counterfactual state of affairs: In each place actually occupied by a feline robot, there was instead a look-alike feline animal, a mammal quite like tigers and pumas, and one with a common ancestry, but smaller and tamer, and so on. Now we ask, "What *would have been* the case if, instead of so many 'deceptive' robots, this *were* the situation; *would there* then have been cats or not?"

My dominant response to this combined thought experiment is distinctly affirmative: Had there been such feline animals, instead of robots, they would indeed have been cats. Moreover, I sense no dominated conflicting tendency. For those not already affected by the causal theory, this response pattern seems rather typical. For the causal theory, that is a very unfortunate result.

In relation to this combined example, the hypothetical feline animals lack the essential features of the actual paradigmatic specimens. For simplicity, suppose that the sample specimens are essentially robots. Then, the hypothetical beings lack the essential robotry. In all events, on the causal theory, 'cat' cannot be projected to the hypothetical animals. If the theory predicts our dominant response, then the response is that these animals are not cats. But that is not the dominant response.

In combined cases, the causal view does not even appear to do at all well. This failure with our third type of case leads us to question whether the causal theory really does well with the cases of the first two types. Indeed, we may doubt whether any *semantic* understanding is so influential and needs to be articulated to that purpose.

C. Troubles from the Past

In subsection A, we considered some examples in which our society was first faced with one sort of thing, say, feline animals of the familiar domestic sort, and then later faced with another sort of thing, say, Martian feline robots, productive of the same appearances to us. In those examples, the earlier items were from now on into our futures. Suppose, now, that we keep the idea of such a temporal shift in the population of target objects, say, in the putative cats, but *move the time of the shift backward* a significant way. Then, we will have examples in which at different past times in our civilization's history we and our ancestors encountered different sorts of objects. In this subsection, I would like to examine a pair of examples that are both of this general sort but that, I think, contrast with each other interestingly.

Consider a *case of five hundred years of recent robotry.* In this example, things are as ordinarily believed up until five hundred years ago: plenty of relevant feline animals around, no feline robots. Then, five hundred years ago, in an undetected flash, the Martians replaced each such animal with a "duplicate" robot (perhaps taking the animals to Mars, where they were not subsequently encountered by any human being). For the past five hundred years, humans have been encountering just such robots, which "inhabit" our planet in the now familiar fashion.

Without protracted reflection upon the case, my dominant response is to think that, relative to this example, *both* the older feline animals *and* the more recent robots are cats. As regards the recent robots, but not as regards the animals, I have a dominated conflicting response as well. But my dominant reaction is "generous" to the recent robots; I accord them the status of cats.

Now, consider a *case of five hundred years of ancient robotry.* This time, we suppose that the period of feline robots is of the same duration, five centuries, but is much farther back in our past. Let us say that it ended five thousand years ago; then, we can call that five-hundred-year period "the time of the baptizers." So, at the end of this baptizer time, each robot was replaced by a "duplicate" feline animal, perhaps bred on Mars from some pumas abducted eons ago. And it is just such animals that we have been encountering and have been considering cats for the past five thousand years.

My dominant response here is that *only the feline animals* are cats, *not* those feline robots. And I sense no dominated, conflicting response in the matter. Notice how different this is from my response to the previous case.

How do these responses bear on the causal theory? Even assuming the customary methodology for examples, the matter is rather complex. That is because there are two different versions of the theory (as well as "compromises" between them) and the responses bear differently on the two versions. First, there is the resolutely *historical* version advocated by Kripke and, at times, endorsed by Putnam. Second, and in contradiction to the first version, there is the (more) *current* version, which Putnam has advanced. Let us consider each version in turn, beginning with the more historical one.

Consider the case of five hundred years of ancient robotry. What does the historical version predict for this example? Well, since the linguistic originators were all encountering (almost) only robots in connection with uses of their (cognate of our) 'cat', *such robots should be the only cats,* the only objects of the sort for which 'cat' and cognates projects. After all, this is not just a few old cases gone awry, or even a bad week for ostending usage; it is five full centuries of nothing but these contraptions all over the earth. So, the causal theory will urge the aforementioned directive, which naturally may be divided thus: (a) such robots as the baptizers encountered *are* cats, and (b) such animals as we later encounter, not being such robots, are *not* cats. In fact, our dominant responses, as noted, are directly opposite *both* as concerns (a) *and* as concerns (b). As far as predicting response goes, the theory fails on both counts here.

Now, let us look at how this version deals with the example concerning *recent* robotry for five hundred years past. Here, the original specimens are all feline animals of the relevant sort; it is just those animals that the baptizers encountered. So, on the historical version, *only such animals should be cats.* This also naturally divides in two: (a) such animals will be cats, and (b) the "duplicate" robots, not being animals, will not be cats. As noted, our dominant response conforms with (a), but it goes *opposite* to (b). As far as predicting responses for this example goes, the historical version scores on one count and fails on the other.

Taking the pair of examples together, as appears natural, the historical causal theory succeeds on one count while failing on three. That is very bad for any theory that would treat philosophical cases, even for one, unlike the causal theory, that might do quite well with so many other examples. Nor is this failure an artifact of chosen specifics, for example, the artificial character of the robotic specimens. Though a bit less marked, very much the same results are obtained with more natural examples: Substitute Martian reptiles for robots; compare metal specimens for 'gold' with wooden ones. Moreover, a natural interstellar wind could do the shifting; no intelligent agentry is required, whether from Mars or elsewhere. As far as its historical version goes, the causal theory for words receives very little support indeed from our actual responses to examples.

Now, let us turn to the current version of the causal theory, the version in which our current semantics is not (much) determined by encounters with objects deep in the past. On this version of the causal theory, the basis for the projection of 'cat' will be the sampled items of our own (recent) social group. So, in both of our examples, the items encountered by humans during the past five centuries will be the basis for projection. For the case of ancient robotry, this version has no problem. Not so in our other case: In the case of recent robotry, only robots are such crucially sampled items. So, on this current version, only robots will be cats; feline animals will not be. But as our dominant responses go, though the recent robots are taken as cats, so are the ancient animals. Indeed, there is a conflicting dominated response with the robots, but there is no such conflict for the animals.[12]

In defense of either version, some will object that these two cases can be handled by declaring that a change occurred in the semantics of 'cat' to mirror the change in the population of encountered objects.[13] But this defense is extremely weak. In the first place, our intuitive thoughts about the examples do not confirm the idea of any such semantic shift and, in fact, actually go the other way. With respect to either of the cases, we can ask whether the older people and the newer had words for putative cats that meant the same or not, that were semantically of a piece or that were disparate. The dominant response, it is clear, is that there was no relevant change from their 'cat' to our 'cat'; rather, our 'cat' will give a (nearly) perfect translation, we respond, of the original cognate. Finally, in responding, we think of their word and ours as being true of exactly the same objects.

In the second place, the assumption of such a semantic shift goes against our more reflective thinking as well. The shift in sample objects, after all, was wholly undetected by any speaker of any relevant language: Each speaker was always under the impression that, in facing such an object, he was encountering an animal. So, what could possibly account for the proposed shift? Moreover, if such a semantic change occurred, *when* did it occur? As we think of candidate times, none seems suitable.

What is determining our responses to these troubling examples concerning the past? Is it a set of beliefs directly reflective of some complex semantic conditions we have internalized? Perhaps so, but then those conditions would seem bizarre as well as complex.[14] Moreover, other examples produce responses that are just as troublesome for the prevalent approach of explaining reactions semantically.[15] With only a bit of ingenuity, the troubles can be seen, I believe, to keep mounting and mounting. But there is no need now to canvass further cases, and perhaps that would even be distracting. For we have enough material already in view to suggest that an alternative approach to our responses might be preferable to, or at least not worse than, the prevalent approach.

3. Some Advantages of a Psychological Approach to Examples

On an appropriately *broad psychological approach*, we need not assume that any semantic understanding must prevail in determining (beliefs that, in turn, determine) responses to an example. Where conflicts are found, as with Putnam's feline robot case, there is a particular call for a complexity of factors: So we look among our beliefs for some to favor each side. We try to spot the simplest, most ordinary contenders, one each to lead the group favoring each side: The stronger of the two salient attitudes favors the dominant response. When that is done, we do not suppose that we have a complete explanation, of course, but we do think that we may have articulated the main elements of the story.

To explain our responses to certain of the more complex examples, the relevant strong beliefs cannot be articulated as being extremely neat and simple. But for the feline robot case, we can have things about as simple as one might please: Productive of the dominant, affirmative response is, simply, the belief that there have been cats, a past-directed *existence* belief as to such ordinary entities; productive of the dominated response is the belief that (if there are cats, then) cats are animals, a *property* belief as to the same sort of entities.

Because our belief that there have been cats is stronger than our belief that cats are animals, both Putnam and I respond to his example dominantly in an affirmative way. If we did not so respond, we would, in effect, be allowing such a hypothetical course of experience to undermine the existence belief, indicating the belief not to be such a strong one for us. Instead, we allow the property belief to be undermined. Nonetheless, since the existence belief is not so very much stronger than the property belief here competing with it, the latter does produce a sensed response as well. The belief that cats are animals loses the staged contest all right, but it is not a shutout. Simple though they be, those are, I suggest, the main lines of the story.

It is instructive to notice our response pattern to related examples. Just as we believe that cats are animals and that cats are not robots, so we believe, too, that cats are mammals and that cats are not green. Suppose, for one case, that all of the presumed mammalian features for cats were not really theirs but were the product of some widespread illusion. Breaking through the illusion, we now discover that all the things taken to be cats have always been reptiles, not mammals at all. If this should be the case, will there have been cats anyway or not? The dominant response is again the affirmative one, of course, but this time I sense no conflict, *no dominated* response to the contrary.

For another case, suppose that the colors we have been attributing to cats, tan and gray and black and so on, have all been the product of widespread illusion: Each animal secretes a substance that distorts perception of its color. Those appearing to be tan secrete one sort of substance; those seeming to be gray surround themselves with another sort of cloud. When the clouds are "seen through," via recently developed techniques for so doing, all these beasts are seen to be pure green. Will these animals actually have been cats? There is an *uncontested* positive response.

On our psychological approach, we can explain the contrasting patterns naturally. The existence belief in cats is *very much* stronger than the property beliefs it saliently contests in these two new cases. The lack of any (sensed) conflict of intuition just indicates this great disparity of strength. By comparison of strength considerations, the belief that cats are animals is stronger than the belief that cats are mammals, and the (negative property) belief that cats are not robots is stronger than the belief that cats are not green.[16]

Before we proceed further, let us notice some advantages of our psychological approach over the prevalent approach that are already apparent. First, we have explained not only the occurrence of the dominant responses but also, where they have occurred, the dominated ones as well. The prevalent approach does not do that. Except by positing factors that "confuse" us and that thus "interfere with the smooth operation of our semantic understanding," there is no way for it to do that. And that way, being *ad hoc,* is not appealing.

Second, even as regards explaining the dominant response, on the new approach we have so far been able to proceed without positing anything semantic or even anything vaguely philosophical or even anything indirectly of such a sort, such as a belief we have, correct or incorrect, as to some semantic features. Of course, for certain further explanations we will posit certain semantic beliefs. But we can go a long way without positing anything so ambitious. On the prevalent approach, we cannot.

Third, the results we have reached, on the psychological approach, are propositions we are half-prepared to endorse anyway. We do not need to think that we have made some interesting (negative) discovery, not even about mundane psychological topics, let alone about objective semantic conditions. On the prevalent approach, our responses quickly seem to become guides to exciting new propositions, at least to exciting denials of semantic proposals traditionally held as true. For at least three reasons, then, our psychological approach seems an appealing alternative to contemporary philosophical practice.

How well will such a psychological approach help us with our more complex examples, those seen to be so troublesome for the causal theory and, perhaps, for any purely semantic account? Now, we cannot expect our explanations to be as simple here as things were with Putnam's case, for these new examples themselves are somewhat more complicated. But perhaps matters can, in each case, be kept simple enough for our approach's appeal to be maintained.

A. The Examples with Disparate Pasts and Futures

First, we will consider the case of feline robots in the past and feline animals in the future. As we will recall, the most typical dominant response is that both the past robots and the future feline animals are cats. In addition, there is our dominated response that those robots are not really cats. The explanation of our responses regarding the past robots is, of course, the same as we gave before for Putnam's example. Well, what are we to say of the positive response for the future animals, a reaction that is apparently without conflict? In addition to the past-directed belief, we have the future-directed existence belief, too, that *there will be* cats. Now, this latter belief may not be so powerful, but, relative to this example, it has no serious competitor; to the contrary, our strongest, most available property beliefs actually line up with it. So, for subjects not influenced by any semantic theory, typically there is, without conflict, the response that the future animals will be cats. (As will also be recalled, for other uncommitted people, there is the response that *only* the animals are cats. For them a different psychological explanation is required, which I will not provide. But on this approach there is plenty of room to do so: Individual differences do require explanatory effort and variety, but they cause no embarrassment.)

Let us consider the inverse case, with past animals and future robots. Here the (dominant) response is that only the past animals are cats. Why is this all that we get now? Well, we again have the very strong past-directed existence belief that there have been cats, which prompts that response for the past animals. But, now, there is no very strong salient property belief to contest it, nothing like a conflicting belief that cats are animals. Therefore, we sense no dominated response this time in relation to the past specimens. Finally, we think that the future robots are *not* cats. Why is that? I suggest that it has little to do with any interesting semantic conditions. Rather, the salient competitors here are my strong property belief that cats are animals and, on the other side, my much weaker future-oriented existence belief that there will be cats. Because the former belief is stronger, we do not dominantly reckon those future robots to be cats. Because it is so very much stronger, we do not even have a dominated response to that generous effect.

On the psychological approach, we are thus enabled to explain discrepant responses that would otherwise be puzzling. For the responses just considered, our explanation rests heavily on the proposition that our relevant past existence belief that there have been cats is very much stronger than our correlative future-oriented belief. But, of course, this proposition is eminently plausible, something we are prepared to endorse anyway. By way of these symmetric examples and our asymmetric responses to them, the psychological approach allows us to confirm this plausible proposition.[17] We are in no way required to import some complicated semantic conditions to reflect the noted asymmetry.

B. The Three Related Types of Examples

As will be remembered, we saw that a puzzling pattern of responses arises with three related types of examples: epistemological, metaphysical, and combined. Let us see how our psychological approach might serve to explain things.

On our approach, the epistemological examples pit strong existence beliefs against powerful property beliefs: for instance, 'There have been cats' against 'Cats are animals'. By way of these examples, it seems, *we regard the existence beliefs as challenged.* Generally, we respond to this challenge by affirming the existence beliefs, by thinking along the lines they urge.

In the metaphysical cases, it does *not* strike us that there is a challenge to our salient existence beliefs. In such cases, we are *given* plenty of relevant objects *as actually existing,* say, plenty of existing cats, and we are asked to describe only some further items that are counterfactual, taken as not existing. In that the relevant existence is given, our strong property beliefs, say, that cats are animals, face no serious competitor. Accordingly, for the further items, they hold sway: If those counterfactual items are not animals, then they are not cats.

Finally, we may easily explain our response to the combined example. Because we will stave off threats to our existence belief as to cats, we judge the "actual" robots to be cats anyway, our property belief that cats are animals thus being overridden. With the "merely counterfactual" mammals, the existence belief has already been satisfied. So, for judgment on them, our property beliefs have no serious competitor. Thus, they determine our response: Those hypothetical entities, being the relevant sort of mammalian animals, are cats, too.

C. The Troubles from the Past

The case of five hundred years of ancient robotry is easy to explain even within the simple format, with the meager resources, so far articulated for our psychological approach. Our response, without conflict, that the feline animals of recent millennia are cats flows both from our existence belief that there have been cats and from our property beliefs as to such entities, notably our belief that cats are animals. Since no strong belief of ours contests the ascription of cathood to the recent candidates, no conflict is present in the matter. As regards the ancient robots, there is, without conflict, the response that they are not cats. But, among the beliefs canvassed, what will support cathood for them? The existence belief will not, for it is already satisfied, made true by all those more recent animals just lately noted. Nor will property beliefs help those items much here. Indeed, the powerful belief that cats are animals operates clearly against them. At least in main outline, the entire response pattern for this case is thus readily accounted.

In contrast, the case of five centuries of recent robotry requires a markedly more complex explanation. The complexity is not required to explain the response, without conflict, for the many feline animals of ancient millennia: that they are cats. That much is easily explained along lines already laid down. The place where complexity is needed is in reference to the feline robots of the past five hundred years.

As will be recalled, the dominant response is that these entities, too, are cats. There is conflict here, we also recall, and the presence of the response that the entities are *not* cats, which happens to be the *dominated* one, is easily accounted: Since our strong property belief is that cats are animals, those robots, which are not animals, are not cats. A problem arises, however, in explaining *why* that response is *dominated*, not dominant. Indeed, the main problem is to explain why there occurs *at all* the response, in fact, even dominant, that those robots are cats.

As responses to other cases indicate, the salient property beliefs mainly speak against these recent items being granted cathood: That "generosity" conflicts with our strong property belief that any cats are animals. What attitude, then, prompts the generous response we make? It cannot be the past existence belief, for our belief that there have been (many) cats (for many hundreds of years) is already satisfied by the many feline animals of the many prior centuries. So what belief might then be responsible?

To complete our explanation, at the present level of inquiry, we need posit only a more specific belief regarding past existence: that there have been (many) cats (on earth) *during the last five hundred years*. This belief is not made true by the ancient animals. The only conspicuous candidates for cathood that will give it that status are the more recent feline robots. So we take those robots to be cats.

This explanation presents no surprises. The specific existence belief introduced is an attitude we are prepared to ascribe anyway and perhaps do ascribe implicitly in everyday life.

Nonetheless, there is the feeling that, unless we can fit this belief into a somewhat detailed and comprehensive pattern, its use in our explanation is not fully motivated. *Why is it*, we ask, that we believe *so very strongly* that there have been cats around for the *last five centuries*, even more strongly than we believe that cats are animals? *Why is it* that we do not believe *anywhere nearly as strongly*, though we, of course, do believe it, that there were cats around during the five centuries of the baptizers?

An adequate answer to these deeper questions, issues that are now forced upon us, requires, I believe, some substantial development of the psychological approach. Let me try to sketch the main lines of the needed development.

4. Perceived Threats to Our System of Beliefs

Many philosophically interesting examples produce conflicting responses. In all of these cases and in some others, too, the person encountering the example is posed with a threat, either way, to his system of beliefs and to the beliefs of his society. A stronger belief will prevail, producing the dominant response indicative of its presence. But what *makes* a belief strong, in the sense of power here in mind? *Why* is the belief that there have been cats stronger than the belief that cats are animals?

We reason implicitly along both lines of choice. We conclude that the failure of the existence belief will present a *greater threat to our whole system of beliefs* than will the failure of that property belief. In outline, how goes this reasoning? A naive view would be that cats are so central to our ontology, our view of what there is and has been, that we cannot readily stand for their existence to be denied. But that is just too naive; it cannot be right. Unlike material objects in general, and perhaps unlike people, cats themselves do not have that importance.

Rather, the reasoning goes like this: If we have been wrong about the existence of cats, what is to stop our having been wrong about dogs and mice, too? And, then, can trees and flowers be far behind; and, then, sticks and stones and chairs and tables? Unless the leak in the dike is plugged quickly, there may occur the undermining of (almost) all our beliefs as to ordinary existence. Our words, and our ideas, for apparently common objects will all fail to apply to reality. Then, we will be completely at sea or floating without even that much of a medium.

To a very great extent, we are better able to tolerate that we have been wrong about the natures of the things we have taken to be plainly there before us. No doubt, there are limits to the tolerance here. But we will not have crossed those lines yet, should we abandon the belief that cats are animals. Such a rejection does *not appear* to involve or to threaten our going down a path to cognitive chaos. (And in matters of quick responses, it is the *appearances* that *count*, not the actual logical, semantic, or epistemic relations.) So, psychologically, matters of ordinary existence are more *main matters for us* than are (almost any) matters as to the natures of common things.

If this hypothesis about reasoning and response is on the right track, then we very strongly believe that our own society has, over a substantial period, *correctly* applied our ordinary words for things. This belief is rather complex: It involves things about people, their words, and the semantic relations of those words to objects. As such, this belief is, no doubt, weaker than the belief that these ordinary entities have existed, whose truth its own must imply. But it is very powerful all the same. And at least as strong are particular beliefs to that general effect— that our society has correctly applied, over much time, 'cat' to many objects: (Almost) whatever the nature of those objects and (almost) whatever the semantics of 'cat', the word is true of many of those cited entities. And quite similar beliefs, we should add, with quite similar strengths concern the reference for various other ordinary words of ours: We believe very strongly that we have correctly applied to many objects our word 'red'; many things called 'red' by us actually are or have been red, (almost) whatever the meaning of 'red' and (almost) whatever the nature of redness and of those objects. These beliefs as to our *correct application* are, it is true, *semantic* beliefs, unlike those beliefs previously cited in our psychological explanations. But these beliefs, though semantic, are not semantically informative in their content. Rather, they are *mute* as to the semantic *conditions* of the words they concern: They offer no semantic characterization whatever.

More pertinent to our main topic, we have such mute semantic beliefs, too, about such common "absolute" terms as 'flat', 'empty', and 'vacuum', not only about 'cat' and 'gold'. These mute beliefs are very powerful. Thus, we confirm the ideas we sketched at the end of the preceding chapter. We *very* strongly believe that many members of our society have encountered objects, for example, fields and tabletops, to which they have *correctly applied* 'flat', our ordinary word. And, of course, the same goes for this word's philosophically more interesting cousins: 'certain', 'know', 'free', 'cause', and so on. For example, we *very* strongly believe that (almost whatever 'know' means and almost whatever is going on in us and the world) many cases in which specific *knowledge* has been attributed by someone in our society are cases in which the attribution has been *correct*.

The main psychological points here, so very general, are, it seems to me, sufficiently important that they cannot be overemphasized: We respond so as to reject the possibility, perceived as ominous, of our words failing in semantic application. We very much care and very strongly believe that our common terms are often true of many things and situations. We very much care and very strongly believe that these terms contribute, in familiar ways, to simple sentences that are true (or that express what is true) and that have been used by us to speak the truth. It is these influential, motivating beliefs, I think, and not the (internalized) understanding of specific semantic conditions, that explains our responses to relevant examples, responses that favor contextualism and favor (more of) common sense. This apparently defensive feature of what we may call our *commonsense system of belief* is one we have just begun to explore.

5. Egocentric Attitudes as Determinants of Response

There is an interesting asymmetry in our responses to the pair of troubling examples about the past. In one case, the five hundred years of *recent* robotry, *my own* social group will be wrong on the matter of semantic application in our uses of 'cat', one of our (fairly) main matters. We will be wrong, that is, unless many robots are cats; so I respond in that way. In the other case, with that much *ancient* robotry, only some *rather distant* group will be wrong, the old baptizers. Not caring so much about their having been right, I deny that their encountered robots were cats, letting them be wrong about whether there were cats around them. Perhaps, then, the asymmetry of response to this pair of examples is to be explained, not semantically, but by an *egocentric bias* in my attitudes toward perceived others. Perhaps all of us have such a bias.

The egocentric bias that I am positing is far from obvious. Rather, it is sensed through the consideration of response patterns to groups of (wildly) hypothetical examples. But though not easy to see, the bias nonetheless might be real.

The tendency I posit will, under appropriate conditions, overcome more commonly observed tendencies that we have. What is such a more easily observed disposition? Well, we have a strong tendency toward taking small, feline, mammalian animals to be cats, and, more to our present point, we have a strong tendency *against* treating as cats a group of things that is very different from them. The greater the perceived difference, the greater the adverse tendency. (So, I am more disposed to exclude robots from cathood than I am reptiles.) But when countervailing psychological forces are at work, these adverse tendencies are sometimes overcome, even the stronger among them. On the psychological approach, we try to characterize these countervailing tendencies and to watch their effective operation.

In general outline, my relevant social attitudes work like this: Some social groups I will favor; some I will not. When I favor some folks, I will try to get their view of the world in touch with (what I take to be) reality. For a favored group, I will treat their 'cat', for example, as being true of so many items encountered by so many members (subject, of course, to some qualifications). For a group that is not so favored, I will be more of a stickler about what cats are supposed to be, even about what 'cat' is supposed to mean.

Which groups will I favor and which groups not? There are several factors, often interacting, that determine my treatment. One factor is how *substantial* the group is perceived to be, itself a complex feature involving several simpler components. But without analysis, the group of all mankind is more substantial than the group of all Africans; the group of all mankind for the past thousand years is more substantial than all of us humans for just the past ten. The more substantial I take a social group to be, the more I favor it.

I want to focus on another determinant, at the heart of my posited egocentric bias. This factor is *the social distance from the perceiver* of the social group in question. When I am the perceiver, the factor becomes the social distance *from me* as I perceive that. When I am in the group, that distance is zero, the minimum. The group of all mankind for the past ten years, and also for the past thousand, is at this minimum social distance from me. The people at the time of the baptizers are at a much greater social distance. The smaller the social distance from me that I perceive for a social group, the more I favor those people. The people for the past five hundred years are a favored group, but not those alive during the time of the baptizers. Because of this, I treat the feline robots of the former group as cats, but not the robots of the latter group. My social attitudes, productive of this responsive treatment, are imbued with favoritism, bias, or prejudice.

The explanation of our responses by such egocentric attitudes is hardly flattering. Consequently, many people will object. Let us see what they might say. Since our space here is limited, we consider only three types of objection. The first two can be treated quickly, but, since the third places our posited bias in an interesting perspective, I shall deal with it at greater length.

First, the noted asymmetry of response to our two examples may be attributed to an asymmetry in the examples themselves, not to any interesting attitudes supposedly revealed by way of the cases. True enough, given our simple presentation of the cases, on the most natural understanding of them, they are not symmetric. In the recent robotry case, there was only *one* salient shift, from animals to robots. In the ancient case, on the other hand, *two* such shifts will be considered: first, from animals to robots and then from robots back to animals. Some may seize on this difference in the examples to explain the discrepancy in response. But that will not do. Either of the cases can be easily altered so that it becomes relevantly symmetric with the other, that other then held constant. Here is just one way: Hold constant the ancient robotry case. For recent robotry, suppose that only a few months ago, after five hundred years of machines, each of the feline robots was instantaneously replaced by a "duplicate" feline animal, perhaps from Mars. (During the past five centuries, we may suppose, the Martians kept breeding such animals on their planet, undetected by humans.) Accordingly, for the past few months, we humans have been encountering only these feline animals, not robots any more. With these suppositions in force, we think of each case as having two shifts in encountered population; the examples are relevantly symmetric now. But there is still the discrepancy of response.

Another attempt to avoid the conclusion of egocentricity proceeds along these lines. The baptizers are a *much less substantial* social group than are the folks of the past five centuries. There are fewer of them, their culture amounts to less, and so on. With this objection, we have noted an important factor influencing our social judgments. But the factor does not seem telling in the case at hand. We may change the example so that the baptizers are numbered in the billions and so that their culture is incredibly advanced: They took space trips to other planets (but did not discover the Martian shenanigans). Our dominant response remains the same.

A third attempt to avoid the egocentric conclusion will involve the presentation of new, related examples in which our responses do *not* seem governed by egocentric attitudes. For instance, suppose that there have been only feline animals everywhere but in New York State, where I was born and raised, where I now live and have spent most of my life, where most of my family comes from, and so on. The Martians, we suppose, perpetrated their robotry, for however many centuries, just in New York. If this is the situation, will these items have been cats anyhow? My dominant response is in the negative. As far as I can tell, I have no more tendency to think these robots to be cats than I would were the example shifted away from my region, so that, say, the robots were always just in Illinois, where my perceived social experience is very slight indeed. If I were egocentric, it might be claimed, there should be a discrepancy in these responses, which there is not.

This line may be taken as well with examples in which social proximity follows time, not space, as in our examples of recent and ancient robotry. For one example of this sort, suppose that the Martian robots had the run of our planet, not for the past five *hundred* years, but for just the past *five* years; otherwise, it has always been the feline animals. To this example of recent robotry my response is that the robots are *not* cats. I sense no tendency to think otherwise. If I were egocentric, it may be said, I would rule those robots to be cats, along with the animals. In that way, I would, after all, minimize the incorrect beliefs about encounters with cats for me and my group, much as I seem to do in our original case of recent robotry, with the five hundred years. But, as noted, I do not seem so egocentric here.

In a rather similar vein, we may suppose a variant on the example of ancient robotry. In this version, there are only feline robots on earth from time immemorial up until fifty years ago, which is well before I was born. Then, a switch was made to small feline animals, to living "duplicates," perhaps bred by Martians from abducted pumas. My dominant response this time is that *both* the older robots as well as the more recent animals are cats. If I were egocentric, it could be said, this would not be my response. Rather, I would reject cathood for the older items, according the status only to the recent animals, the specimens within my own lifetime.

Our third objection involved three examples. To each of these examples, my dominant response was not an egocentric one, not well explained by positing any such bias. But what does that show? Does it show that there really is no egocentric tendency in my system of attitudes? No, it does not. For there are other examples, we have observed, that do indicate such a tendency in me. Well, then, how can we reconcile the various indications of these two groups of examples? The reconciliation is easily affected: As some examples indicate, my social attitudes do have an egocentric bias. But, as other examples also indicate, this bias is *not* a *narrow* one; rather, it operates only in the large. Though I am prejudiced to favor my own, my prejudice is a rather cosmopolitan one. The earlier of our examples indicates that there *is* a prejudice; the three later examples indicate *limits* of the prejudice.

Within cosmopolitan limits, the various psychological factors work together to produce my social judgments. By way of certain social judgments, I will consider certain objects cats; by way of others, less favorable, I will treat other candidates differently. In large measure, this is a matter of *degree*. So, along lines already laid down, we can produce an infinite spectrum of cases and notice increasing, and decreasing, tendencies in responsive judgments. As a five-hundred-year period and its people get closer to me now, I increasingly tend to judge its feline robots to be cats. As such a group moves farther away from me, if only in my imaginative suppositions, there is a decreasing tendency toward favorable judgment.

These variable tendencies are not, I believe, importantly related to the semantics of 'cat' or of any other expression. To stick with accepted methodology and suppose otherwise is, I suggest, to become party to doubtful contentions about our language.

Suppose, contrary to my position, that our responses are to be accounted for by correct semantic understanding. Then, our pattern of responses to these examples indicates that each person is, in an important way, the reference point for determining what is what, for example, for determining what is a cat and what is not. After all, as my responses go, what counts as a cat is *in relation to* the word uses and specimen encounters of *favored* substantial groups. And the large social groups thus favored are, as my responses go, those socially close enough to *me*. So, although indirectly, what 'cat' is true of, and thus *what things are cats*, is determined largely by the relation of many specimens to *me*, Peter Unger. But, for two related reasons, this is doubtful.

In the first place, even as I can tell, I am *just not that important*. Which things are cats, which fishes, which roses—none of these are matters that revolve around Peter Unger. Though I sometimes overestimate my own importance, on these matters not even I can think otherwise; I certainly do not expect anyone else to do so.

Second, taking these responses as semantically informative promotes an *unwanted semantic subjectivism*. For just as my own responses will then indicate such supreme importance for me, so anyone else's will indicate the same exalted position for him or for her. For instance, if he bothered to examine such examples and his responses to them, David Hume should conclude as much for himself. Since he lived so much earlier than I, the reference point he determines, or which he is, will be notably different from the one I am. Now, his 'cat', I submit, will not be true of so many different possible objects than mine is; rather, we share one word, true of just the same objects, or at least very nearly the same, no matter who employs it.

A cautious treatment of these matters suggests a broadly psychological approach, not a directly semantic one: Whatever the positive features of our language, it is doubtful that they conspire to give each of us the impression that he, and he alone, is the measure of all things. Perhaps, as our responses to examples suggest, each of us has deep attitudes to such an egocentric effect. But that is a matter of our individual psychologies, including our socially oriented attitudes, and not of the language itself in which those attitudes, along with so much else, might find some expression.

Because this chapter is to a considerable degree an examination of the causal theory for words, it is almost obligatory for me to make at least very brief mention of Putnam's celebrated Twin Earth cases.[18] For it is thought by many that cases of this type provide genuine, important support for the causal theory for words. But such a thought requires, I suggest, taking only a quick and narrow view. When more and more Twin Earth examples are examined, as I have elsewhere done in some detail, troubles quickly set in for the theory and even for the prevalent methodology essential for the view's appeal.[19] Examples that seem devastating to the theory and appear to require bizarre semantic understanding on the prevalent approach are easily explicable in terms of egocentric attitudes of just the sort we have lately observed. Almost as a matter of course, the more usual Twin Earth cases are also well explained within the framework of our broad psychological approach. So much, then, for the causal theory of reference for common words, initially implausible and, after all, deeply troubled no matter which methodological approach is adopted.

The next section focuses on issues more directly relevant to the main theme of our essay.

6. Ostensible Intuitions, Commonsense Beliefs, and Semantic Relativity

If our psychological approach is superior to the prevalent approach, as we have been arguing, then we have a direct reply to the objection from semantic intuitions: Our responses to many examples are only ostensibly indicative of semantic understanding and are actually informative only as to certain strong commonsense beliefs not generated by, or directly related to, any internalized semantic conditions. This claim is true, or true enough, not only as regards responses to hypothetical cases, mild as well as wild, but also as regards reactions to actual situations. The claim is true, or true enough, not only as regards the specification of whatever determinate conditions certain words may have, but also as regards the question of whether certain words have determinate conditions in the first place. In particular, as we have hypothesized, this may well be going on with responses to actual cases, and to many hypothetical cases, involving the alleged flatness of physical surfaces. Our positive response, that 'flat' does apply and so has conditions fit for application, may be no real indication of any such state of affairs. It may only indicate how very strong is our belief that this common word does semantically apply to common physical realities and how strong, too, is our belief that we have correctly applied the word to many ordinary physical objects in many encounters. The chain of implicit reasoning sketched near the end of the preceding chapter is, it appears, firmly anchored in very powerful commonsense beliefs, but beliefs that are mute as to the status of, and the character of, alleged semantic conditions.

If our psychological approach is superior, then, the objection from semantic intuitions is badly misconceived and will, in fact, reduce to this: The proposition that 'flat' and so many other conjectured terms actually are true of many objects is more in keeping with (more of) common sense than is any proposition that contradicts it. What the objection boils down to is that, on the whole, the hypothesis of semantic relativity, which is one such contradictor, conflicts with our commonsense system of beliefs. But, since this much was acknowledged at the outset, the objection from semantic intuitions means no new problem for the relativity hypothesis.

Suppose, now, that, for all our argumentation, the psychological approach is *not* superior to the prevalent approach. Now, as indicated earlier, it does not follow from this supposition that the psychological approach is an inferior mode of treatment. For we must consider a third alternative: that neither approach is objectively superior to the other, that there is no fact of the matter as to what is the most accurate approach to account for our cognitive responses.

Especially supposing the psychological approach lacks objective superiority, this alternative is no mere logical possibility. Given that supposition, it is fairly plausible to suppose that it will obtain. Reconsider the various explanations of response we have given in our treatment of the causal theory and its counter-examples. The prevalent approach, in such cases, will lead us to postulate very complex semantics for many terms and very complex acts of semantic grasping in our total psychology. The psychological approach has all of that be much simpler. But, on the other hand, the prevalent approach does seem, in obvious ways, to be a simpler methodology than does the psychological approach. And, along with that, it seems that on the prevalent approach the *rest* of one's attributed psychology will be somewhat simpler. Now, as I have been arguing before, I do not think that the gain in simplicity just indicated is so great as to offset the much more complex semantics that seems required. But maybe it is; maybe, despite appearances, I have unduly favored the psychological approach. Such a proposition is, I am afraid, at least moderately plausible: Each approach has advantages that offset its disadvantages and, thus, offset the advantages of the other. What then? Well, in such an event, the likely situation is, I think, this: The total account of response one arrives at by following the prevalent approach will be no worse than, but also no better than, that obtained by following the psychological approach. Then, there will be no fact of the matter as to what approach is correct to take toward our responses to examples. This is entirely congenial to, even virtually equivalent to, the hypothesis of semantic relativity.

Of the three logically possible alternatives in the area, as this area has been defined here, the only one sufficient to give real force to the objection from semantic intuitions is the third: that the prevalent approach is objectively superior to the psychological approach. Although I have not conclusively ruled out this last proposition, which is doubtless beyond human power to do, the burden of argument now goes against it. Therefore, the burden rests on the shoulders of one who would press on with the objection from semantic intuitions.

Though stemming from an approach that is widely popular, as an independent charge the objection from semantic intuitions may be discounted, at least for the foreseeable future. But what of the proposition to which, as I said, this misplaced charge boils down: that semantic relativity conflicts with (most of) our commonsense beliefs in the area? When a hypothesis does that, we almost always are disinclined to believe that hypothesis. And this reluctance on our part does not seem at all irrational. Does all of this present much difficulty to our hypothesis of semantic relativity and so, too, to our hypothesis of philosophical relativity? For two related reasons, I do not think so.

My main reason is really very simple; I need offer only a reminder, no newly argued idea: It is not my claim that we should believe the hypotheses for which I am arguing, nor is it my intention to produce in anyone so positive an attitude toward these conjectured propositions. On the contrary, my aims and claims are much more modest: We should not reject these hypotheses altogether, but, despite their initial strangeness, we should take them quite seriously as having some significant chance of proving true or true enough. We should treat these proposals as things that some day, though almost certainly not very soon, we might actually come to believe or to accept quite fully. Such a day, if ever it comes to pass, will be one when we have a much deeper and fuller understanding of language, of thought, and of the relations between them and when this understanding makes clear what is now still at best obscure—the adequacy of the relativity hypotheses. Now, such a very mildly positive attitude toward these conjectures is, it should be clear, completely compatible with a very great deal of respect for, and with even a very strong allegiance to, our commonsense thinking.

My subsidiary reason involves something in the way of reminders but also something in the way of new observation. For our commonsense beliefs involve, I now want to observe, not only various inconsistencies but also various other unattractive features. By way of reminder, we may point to this inconsistency in the neighborhood of our main topic: Many of our terms, such as 'flat', will (according to common sense) both be invested with semantics relevantly *independent of* temporary conversational concerns and be used in a wide variety of contexts to make positive statements that are true, the truth *depending on* current conversational interests. This point was discussed in chapter II, section 7. By way of new observation, we may say that an unattractive feature of another sort is this: There is governing our commonsense attitudinal system an egocentric bias that is at least somewhat less than fully rational.[20] Now, a system of beliefs with such features as these will, for philosophical purposes, require some substantial revamping, even if most of the system should survive the reconstruction. Perhaps various main aspects of common sense will, upon proper consideration, one day be abandoned, and not at all irrationally. And perhaps these aspects will include, or should include, those attitudes of ours that, as of now, bar us from believing in the relativity hypotheses. We should, I suggest, seriously consider the possibility.

VI

The Status
of Philosophical Problems

There are, I believe, two main sorts of charge against our hypothesis of philosophical relativity. One of these, the objection from semantic intuitions, is available only to the philosopher of common sense, not to his traditional skeptical opponent. In the two chapters just preceding, we have dealt with this charge well enough, I think, for our present purposes.

The other main sort of charge remains to be examined and, perhaps, disarmed. We call this charge, which arises in several forms, the *objection from superficiality:* The hypothesis of philosophical relativity treats certain philosophical problems quite superficially, whereas in fact these problems, which are themselves deep issues, require a more profound treatment. Now, unlike the objection from semantic intuitions, this charge can be brought against philosophical relativity by the traditional skeptical philosopher as well as by his diametric opposite, the philosopher of common sense. As a related point, we may notice that the charge of superficiality seems appropriate only to the more ambitious of our two relativity hypotheses: Although it appears apt for use against the hypothesis of philosophical relativity, it does not seem so apt against the hypothesis of semantic relativity.

A distinct though closely related objection to our approach is that we must view (many) philosophical problems as pseudoproblems, not as genuine difficulties at all. This related charge, it is apparent, is also one available to the traditional skeptic as much as to his commonsense opponent. Unlike the superficiality charge just mentioned, however, this objection does apply to our thesis of semantic relativity quite generally, not just to its philosophically salient applications and the philosophical relativities they seem to generate. But I believe that an adequate reply to the charge of superficiality will serve as well to

105

rebut this closely related charge of pseudoproblems. Therefore, at least in the main, I will address directly only the complaint that our relativistic approach treats philosophical problems in too superficial a manner.

Now, perhaps there is a sense of the term 'problem' according to which the existence of a problem requires there to be some objective answer or solution to that problem: Otherwise, there will not have been a genuine problem there, but only (some factors producing) a misleading appearance of a problem. As a matter of course, in such a sense our relativity hypotheses will indeed imply that certain things taken to be philosophical problems are not really problems at all, let alone problems of much depth. But, if there is such a sense, then, I believe, it is not the only sense of 'problem' as we use it. Moreover, if, most doubtfully, that should be the only sense in use, then we may employ the word as a convenient term of art, abandoning the requirement of an objective answer.

In any event, there are matters in this neighborhood needing to be discussed and ways for us to discuss them (whether the ways be already available or whether readily invented). In whatever terms seem most convenient, we will try to examine the objection from superficiality in all the main forms in which it arises. While trying to be as fair to the objection as we can be, we will attempt to say, clearly enough, why all of its main forms fail.

Suppose that the objections to the relativities—in particular, to the hypothesis of philosophical relativity—can all be disarmed. Suppose, further, that the reason for this is that there is no truer proposition in the topic area than this hypothesis. Then, a large question will press upon us: What philosophical tasks remain on which philosophers might fruitfully expend their intellectual energy? In other words, if the hypothesis of philosophical relativity should be correct or is even on the right track, then in what state does it leave philosophy? After replying to the objection from superficiality, I will try to address this related question.

1. An Objection from Particular Expressions

The first form of the superficiality charge can be called the *objection from particular expressions*. On this objection, our treatment reduces a philosophical problem to one whose semantic aspect is exhausted by disagreements concerning a particular, specific form of expression or else a very few such locutions. An example would be our treatment of the problem of knowledge: On our treatment of this problem, its semantic aspect concerns the word 'know' or sentences of the form 'S knows that p', and very little else in the language. But anything deserving of the appellation "problem of knowledge" will concern not only knowing itself but also justification for belief, reasons for being confident, and many other related matters. The semantic aspect of such a problem, as the issue is more fairly assessed, will include the conditions of 'justification', 'reason', and many other expressions, not just 'know' and its cognates. These wider semantic matters, the objection continues, cannot be encompassed by any debate between contextualism and invariantism or given a plausible relativistic treatment. So, the thesis of philosophical relativity does not apply to a problem of knowledge that is properly philosophical.

I have presented this objection in terms of that problem, among those discussed, to which a reply from us is most difficult. Before we essay such a reply, let us consider the situation with the other problems, where matters are easier for us.

Consider the problem of determinism's consequences. Should someone object that we have reduced this to a problem about 'can', our reply is almost immediate: In perfect parallel with sentences containing 'can', we get objectively undecidable disputes for sentences with 'able', 'power', 'free', and so on. Any means we have for putting the point, not just the particular one lit upon by our objector, generates the division between contextualist and invariantist. If everything that happens is inevitable, are we ever *able* to do something we do not; is it in our *power*, is it *up* to us; are we *free* to do it? If any one of these questions is objectively undecidable, as it appears, then all are. Indeed, decidable or not, they stand or fall together. And all of these questions, and others parallel to them, do encompass a properly philosophical problem of determinism's consequences.

Consider our problem of causation. Should someone object that we have reduced this to a problem about the word 'cause', noun and verb, our reply is again almost immediate: In perfect parallel with sentences containing 'cause', we get interminable disputes for sentences with other expressions to anything like the same effect: Did the drunken driving cause the accident, or was it the road's condition? It cannot be both; or can it? Similarly, did the driving or the condition of the road *make it happen* that there was that accident or *bring about* the accident? Doubts about our singular causal judgments will carry over, just as many or just as few, to doubts about judgments to similar effect. So, our problem of causal judgments is not overly particular in its semantic aspect; rather, it has the earmarks of a properly philosophical difficulty.[1]

What happens with explanation? If we never do explain phenomena, then we never *give an account* of those phenomena, nor do we do anything else to the same desired effect. If there is no fact of the matter as to whether or not we explain, then anything in the same neighborhood is also indeterminate.

Considerations of parallels disarm this objection as regards various problems we have tried to treat. But they do not do much as regards the problem of knowledge: There is no such parallel between 'know', on the one side, and, on the other, 'justified in believing' or 'reasonable for S to believe'. Another sort of reply is required.

We can reply, I think, from considerations of entailment, or semantic requirement. For example, we can argue that, if a person knows nothing to be so, then there is no stock of items to serve as reasons for him, either in action or in belief. If S is reasonable in believing that p, then something must be his *reason* for believing it, say, that q. And, if S's reason is that q, then S must *know* that q. A similar line holds for S's being justified and having genuine justification. So, if people do not *know some* things to be so, then they will not be reasonable or justified, in believing anything at all. The one matter depends upon the other.[2]

This is just one way that lines of entailment can be charted from matters of reason and justification to matters of knowledge. Elsewhere I have argued for others.[3] I suggest that still others can be articulated. Insofar as belief is reasonable or justified or rational, at the center of one's web of belief some knowledge must lie.

Indirectly, but nonetheless for all that, disputes about reasonableness and kin involve debates about knowing, both at the semantic level and at the substantive one. Accordingly, a thesis that the latter debates are objectively undecidable is one that addresses a properly philosophical problem of knowledge. Even in this difficult problem area, then, the hypothesis of philosophical relativity is not defeated by the objection from particular expressions.

But perhaps these matters are not as straightforward as I have indicated: Well before arguing for his thesis of indeterminacy, W. V. Quine objected to the idea that there was any substance to claims of relations of meaning or of semantic requirement.[4] At least he objected to such claims of this sort as the ones I have just been making. On this objection, there will be, in particular, no semantic requirement of any knowledge for statements as to reasonable belief. Since Quine's general challenge is so prominent and since we have been influenced here so much by other aspects of his philosophy, it is only fitting that I say something now about his noted semantic skepticism and, in particular, about how it might or might not bear on the objection from particular expressions.

Are there valid claims about relations of meaning? As H. P. Grice and P. F. Strawson have observed, the burden of argument is surely on Quine, not on the claims and distinctions he challenges.[5] For many of these claims are part of our commonsense belief structure and are, indeed, at least fairly central to the system: An example is the commonly believed claim that it is *inconsistent* (to assert) that someone *knows* that copper conducts electricity and that copper does *not*. Moreover, as Quine's critics have argued, and as we might argue further, Quine has not fully shifted this burden.[6] So, in light of Quine's writings, though we do well to eye our claims of semantic requirement with a certain amount of healthy suspicion, we can still continue to believe in quite a few of these claims.

But suppose that one does not so believe. In such a case, one could still answer the objection from particular expressions, though in a somewhat different fashion. As concerns the problem of knowledge, one could now say this: The relation between knowledge, on the one hand, and reasonable believing, on the other, is not so close as philosophers have supposed. For quite generally, then, with this matter being just one instance, there is not the very close sort of connection among our ideas as has been so often assumed in philosophy (and in common sense as well). Thus, the problem of knowledge is one thing, so to speak, while a problem of reasonable belief is something else again. Our relativistic approach will apply at least to the first of these problems, even if, perhaps, not to the rather different problem that, in this Quinean light, the second appears to be. We never claimed, after all, that our relativity hypotheses would apply to all philosophical problems whatever. And, if Quine is right about the (allegedly looser and inferior) connections among our terms and ideas, we should, as we can, expect a somewhat narrower domain for our relativities.

But, even if Quine is right in these matters, the domain will still look to be plenty wide enough. For in claiming parallel treatments for, say, 'cause', 'make happen', and 'bring about', we nowhere claimed, or needed to claim, any relations of meaning among these expressions or among the relevant sentences continuing them. The relativity approach can be taken to each of the expressions right from scratch, done one at a time, until the area of thought they serve (perhaps variously) to express is saturated with relativistic considerations. Similarly, suppose that there are no semantic connections between (relevant sentences with) 'knows that', 'is aware that', 'is cognizant of the fact that', and so on. Then, one expression at a time, we can saturate with relativity the topic area of "knowledge" by taking each locution in turn as an instance of semantic relativity.

True enough, if Quine is wrong about semantic connections, as I suspect him to be, then we will have *more* to say against the objection from particular expressions, and more ways of saying it. But, even if he is right, it should now be clear, there is quite enough that we may readily bring against this form of the superficiality charge.

The charge of particular expressions tried to make our relativistic approach seem superficial. It tried this by attempting to make the approach seem too narrow to encompass problems of philosophical scope. With that attempt a failure, our relativity hypotheses seem more challenging than ever in at least two important ways.

First, we recall the limited justification we gave for the rationality of our commonsense practice of contextualist attribution of a language to ourselves: Since there is no objective fact of the matter to be decided, it is rational for us to stick with the prevalent procedure already familiar. But (supposing Quine wrong about relations of meaning) we may now sense a question as to the semantics of 'rational', proposed by an invariantist, even as the word occurs in this apparently mild principle. Saying that such a conservative practice is rational for us, this semanticist may reply, logically implies that we *know something* to be so, which grounds the judgment of rationality. On the invariantist alternative, however, it seems that we might not know anything. Therefore, the claim of contextualism's greater rationality, even a modest one, begs the question against its salient competitor.

I am unsure how to assess this invariantist challenge, which to me seems rather a deep one. Perhaps the circularity charged against our claim for contextualism is genuine but not vicious. Then, relative to the contextualist approach, which is dominantly our practiced approach, the position is rational for us. That may be the most we can expect here, but perhaps enough to satisfy. Or perhaps the circularity is more vicious, enough to undermine even the mildest rational preference for contextualist ascription. As I said, I am not sure how deeply our relativity cuts into the matter.

Second, we recall our discussion of the allegedly independent semantics of 'flat', 'certain', and 'cause'. One thing that we conjectured there was this: For (almost) any subject matter, we must have *some* terms, though we may not be sure just which, whose semantic conditions do not depend on the temporary interests of those employing the expressions. Otherwise, there seems no basis for any genuine discussion of a subject matter; the presumed topic seems swallowed up by our own expedient concerns. But it is just this suggestion that seems to have happened in the topic areas we have been discussing: the area of knowledge and anything importantly like it, the area of causation and anything relevantly like it. I find this problem, *the problem of an independent semantic basis*, to be unsettling. Though not in publication, David Lewis suggests that we might not need any such independent terms for a genuine discussion of a subject area: It might be sufficient that what dependence there is, of the terms employed on the temporary interests of the users, should not affect the particular matter being discussed. Perhaps the fleeting concerns can somehow be factored out and then discounted. This suggestion, though sketchy, is intriguing. Can it be developed so that our problem of an independent basis can be dissolved? Again, I am uncertain.

2. An Objection from a Particular Language

When one disputes about the semantics of 'know' or 'cause', one argues about the conditions of a term of one particular human language, of English. But a genuine philosophical problem of knowledge or of causation should not be tied so closely to one language. Either there is *very* much more to such a problem than its semantic aspect or else the semantic aspect of the problem is far greater than the present approach begins to allow. In either case, by making much depend upon words specific to English, the present approach does not do justice to philosophical problems; rather, it makes them appear too provincial. How can we reply to this *objection from a particular language*?

We can respond partly in one way and partly in quite a different way. On the one hand, our approach does not imply that the problems discussed are very provincial. And, on the other hand, these philosophical problems might not be quite as universal as one might think. Let me explain.

Our approach does not make problems more provincial than they are. To be sure, philosophical problems have a semantic aspect; part of the problem concerns the meaning or the conditions of those expressions by means of which people think about the problem. And, generally, the words used by speakers of different languages will differ. But the words used by a speaker of one language may translate quite well those used by a speaker of another. The conditions of my 'know' may be the same as those of the Spaniard's 'saber', or very nearly the same. If that is so, then disputes about my 'know' will parallel debates about 'saber'. There will be a contextualist account of both words and an invariantist account, and there will be (the hypothesis of) semantic relativity for both the English and the Spanish expressions.

On the other side, our philosophical problems might not be universal. Suppose that there is a natural language somewhere, even a very rich one, that contains no expression suitable to translate my 'know'. Perhaps that may be.[7] Will the speakers of that language have a problem of knowledge? I do not see that they will. Indeed, I cannot see how they will think about *knowledge* at all. To this extent, philosophical problems are relative to the languages in which they are formulated; they arise only in languages in which they can be expressed. But even if they may not be universal, may not be issues for all philosophically reflective beings, I do not think this would mean that our philosophical problems are provincial.

Let us agree that matters of translation are matters of degree. Then, the Spanish 'saber' and the English 'know' translate each other to a very high degree; the translations are very good. Suppose that the Venusian 'plutz', their nearest equivalent, translates our 'know' very poorly (and vice versa). Then, we can say, without harmful exaggeration, that we share the semantics with the Spaniards but not with the Venusians. We draw the line. Having drawn it, we can say what we have said: We share a problem of knowledge with the Spaniards but not with the Venusians. Whatever philosophical problems the latter have may include some rather *like* our problem of knowledge but not that problem itself.

Suppose there are some other people, say, Zulus, whose nearest equivalent translates our 'know' not badly, as in the Venusian case, but not well either. There is no plausible line to draw here: Perhaps we cannot say that our terms translate each other and also cannot say that they fail. Let us suppose that this is so. Then, there may be no fact of the matter whether or not such Zulus share with us a philosophical problem of knowledge. But that also does not mean that the relativistic approach makes our problem of knowledge appear overly narrow or superficial.

As many philosophers do, our approach sees an intimate connection between one's language and the more complex thinking that one does, including one's philosophical thinking. But, just as is the case with these philosophers, our approach does not therefore imply that philosophical problems are narrow issues. Now, unlike (at least) most of these philosophers, our approach affirms that the problems are literally unanswerable. Must this be a fault in our treatment? To suppose so now will not do; an adequately discriminating argument is required. But, as far as I can tell, there is nowhere available any such powerful and pointed piece of reasoning.

3. An Objection from Overgeneralization

The preceding objections charged our approach with being too specific and, thus, too limiting. Another objection goes in the other direction, charging us with taking in too much. This is the *objection from overgeneralization*.

On our account, the objection runs, the semantic difficulties with philosophically important terms are of a piece with those for many expressions whose philosophical importance is slight or nil. Semantically, we place 'know' and 'cause' and 'certain' on a par with such absolute terms as 'flat' and 'empty' and 'dry', and perhaps even with such sentences as 'Three people came to town this morning'. Because semantic relativity applies to all of these expressions alike, it reduces the philosophically important expressions to the level of the others. This seems quite improper. Rather, there must be important semantic differences between the expressions.

Without some such differences, the objection continues, there will be an unbridgeable gap between the semantics and substantive philosophy. In such an event, we will have to do much more than just recognize a difference between the two; we will have to deny any significant connection. For, otherwise, there will be, quite on a par with a problem of knowledge, a philosophical problem of, say, *dryness*. And, surely, that takes things too far.[8]

Since that does take things too far, let us go back a few steps. Does our thesis of semantic relativity imply that there is scarcely any semantic difference between those terms deemed philosophically important and those expressions considered otherwise? I do not think so. Our thesis does say that there is a crucial similarity in these expressions, a certain indeterminacy that allows diverse accounts to be equally appropriate. But this similarity may *coexist with* many semantic differences. Because of some of these differences, some of the undecidable terms may be philosophically important and others not.

Let me buttress my point by way of a parallel. Consider ordinary vagueness, the sort of vagueness that encourages sorites arguments, reasoning down slippery slopes. This vagueness might mean a semantic difficulty, perhaps even a sort of semantic indeterminacy, for those expressions it attends. Certain expressions that have this vagueness are deemed philosophically important: 'good' and 'bad'. Others are considered unimportant: 'short' and 'tall'. Now, in addition to the problem of sorites vagueness, which happen to attend the word 'good', there is a philosophical problem of goodness, of the good. But, apart from vagueness, it is absurd to propound as a significant part of philosophy a problem of shortness or a problem of tallness.

Those who recognize the similarity of vagueness for 'good' and 'short' need not say that these terms are semantically alike in all respects. Among the semantic respects in which they differ may be some that account for the fact that 'good' is quite directly suitable for discussion of a philosophically important topic, values, but 'short' is not similarly suitable for discussion of a comparably important topic. Our relativistic theses no more overgeneralize things, I submit, than do those who take seriously the (more) ordinary vagueness found with so many of our everyday expressions.

As far as it goes, the foregoing reply is, I think, a rather good one. But I do not think it goes as far as one should desire. We need to say at least a bit more. Let me explain.

If the semantic features responsible for indeterminacy of philosophically key terms help to explain the interminability of debates about the matters these terms express, as we have contended, then there should be something philosophically more significant *involved in* the indeterminacy of, say, 'know', than in that of, say, 'dry'. But there is. For example, the indeterminacy of 'know' concerns the extent to which, absolute or contextually relative, an agent is in a position to exclude propositions in conflict with a given one. The indeterminacy of 'dry', in contrast, concerns only the extent to which, absolute or contextually relative, liquid, moisture, and suchlike are excluded from a region. The former matter of exclusion is manifestly of greater philosophical interest than is the latter. Accordingly, such indeterminacy as is involved in assessing the (sufficiency of the) range of competing alternatives is bound to be of greater philosophical interest than such as in involved in assessing the (sufficiency of the) liquid to be excluded.

4. An Objection from Unnaturalness

The hypothesis of philosophical relativity is unnatural to try to adopt, often even to contemplate. Now, our position with respect to venerable philosophical problems ought not to be such an unnatural one. For it is natural for us to contemplate these problems and to take them as being objectively answerable. Probably, a sufficiently deep treatment of the problems would harmonize with these natural tendencies. So, probably, a relativistic treatment is too superficial and, thus, an inadequate approach to these problems.

Well, what can one say to such an objection? Trite truths come to mind first:

What has seemed natural at one time seems less natural at other times, and the apparently unnatural often enough becomes natural enough for us. In other areas, views initially downright repugnant became second nature. Why not here, too?

In any event, as we must remind ourselves, our present (and past) situation in this area is scarcely a comfortable one. Let us notice the various aspects of this uncomfortable situation and try to discern the relations among them.

Even discounting considerations of relativity and indeterminacy, there are difficulties attending the philosophically important terms central to the problems under discussion. We have already mentioned one that seems to concern us all quite a bit: On the one hand, we want the semantics of words such as 'cause' and 'knows' to be relevantly independent, free of temporary conversational interests. We believe that this is so but also want it to be. For we want, as we are inclined to believe them to be, questions of knowledge and of causation to be objective matters in that sense or way. But, if the semantics of those words is thus independent of our variable interests, then the terms will never or hardly ever figure in simple positive truths that people actually put forth. And we also desire, indeed, even more strongly that these terms should often be used by us to speak the plain truth. Though common sense would seem to let us have our cake and eat it in these matters, in fact, we cannot possibly have it both ways. So, there is a genuine conflict here for us, one that involves our concerns.

Now, the same general situation, it is true, also occurs with terms that are not of much philosophical interest; 'flat' has been our most often used example. Even with such less interesting terms, we would like to have it both ways but cannot possibly do so. There is this difference: Since 'flat' is (typically) used to discuss matters less central to our deepest concerns than 'knows' or 'free' is, we do not care so much about the pickle we are in with the first of these three expressions. There is the same basic conflict with all of the terms; with those that are more interesting philosophically, the conflict simply bothers us more.

That there might be *indeterminacy* in the semantics of the terms involved in this conflict is an *additional* point about the expressions. That their semantics, and the topics for whose discussion they are central, might be objectively undecidable is, thus, an additional matter.

Perhaps the most interesting point about this whole situation is one that presupposes all of the foregoing points but goes beyond them: The way in which our philosophically important terms are indeterminate *dovetails with* the poignant conflict over these terms that is implicit in common sense, that is there to bother us anyhow. What does this mean? It means that there is no objective way to decide which arm of our dilemma represents the true, or even the truer, position. Which side we most prefer will, I suggest, be only a matter of psychological cost and economy, subjectively assessed.

On the whole, we prefer the commonsense positions on our problems, not their skeptical opposites. But whichever of the semantic options we favor, and thus their object-level "counterparts," we feel unsatisfied; inevitably, we will feel as though something is missing. Habitually, we incline more toward the option that leaves us feeling less so. Our intellectual habits serve to minimize but not to remove our intellectual discomfort.

In other areas of endeavor, life often presents us with such unsatisfying choices. So it is also in philosophy, if not always, then often enough. Enough for what? Enough for us to consider as fairly natural our dilemma of common sense and our lack of a ground on which to resolve objectively this uncomfortable dilemma.

5. Prospects for Philosophy

Relativity holds sway, we have argued, over a significant range of philosophical problems. If this is so, then what have philosophers left to do that requires intellectual effort and may yield philosophical profit? What is the philosophical situation?

In the first place, it must be remembered that it was nowhere claimed or argued that relativity holds sway over all traditional philosophical problem areas, or even over most. No doubt, there will be relativity in more than just the four areas we explored in chapter III. But there may be many areas whose key terms do not generate apparent disputes between contextualist and invariantist. The metaphysical problem of universals would appear a case in point. In those areas, there is no reason to suspect semantic relativity. Then, as far as I can tell, philosophical relativity will be beside the point. For philosophers engaged in such untouched philosophical areas, intellectual life will proceed as usual.

Even a very large domain for business as usual need not, however, be any great cause for feelings of relief, let alone optimism. For the debates in (virtually) all of the central areas of philosophy have gone on for very many years, with little progress achieved in getting us to perceive any offered solution as adequate. I offer no general analysis of this apparently gloomy situation, though, as I said near the outset, I suspect a plurality of preventative factors. Enough of these factors will, no doubt, still be at work in such a domain. At any rate, our relativity position will not make matters any worse there, for it will not affect those areas at all.

More pertinently, what will the situation be like in the problem areas infected or endowed with relativity? Will there be much philosophizing left to do?

It is easy to think, unreflectively, that the discovery of relativity in an area, if a genuine finding, will make for an easy situation, will allow for quick solutions though rather shallow ones. If relativity has been encouraging interminable debates over undecidable issues, then the appreciation of it might cause those debates fruitfully to cease: The disputants will realize that they have been talking at cross-purposes, so to speak, and have never had any genuine disagreement at all. A traditional skeptical philosopher can then work out, in detail, those conventions the adoption of which will have one speak an invariantist language or at least such an invariantist language fragment as will cover the problem area of his concern. He might, for example, work out those conventions that will give invariant determinate meaning to 'know', and by semantic relations already in force, thus also to 'justification' and 'reason'. Then, he will have meanings that will ensure the literal truth of *some* sort of skepticism in epistemology. A philosopher of common sense, in contrast, can work out the details of contextualist conventions for these terms of interest. With the determinate meanings assigned in that direction, some sort of commonsensical view in epistemology will be strongly furthered, if not absolutely ensured. In the infected problem areas, then, there will only be the working out of details for such incomplete, and perhaps complementary, conditional solutions. Though more than logic chopping, it may be granted, this detailed work lacks the depth that one wants from philosophy. In an area in which there is relativity, this seems all that there is left to do.

This line of thinking is as inadequate as it is unreflective. In the first place, the detailed working out of the indicated conventions might be, not only very difficult to do well, but a source of philosophical surprise and even insight. Who can say, in advance, all that we must specify to gain expressions, for a given problem area, that are entirely free of the user's temporary concerns? So, except for the fact that their semantics will be impossibly demanding, who can say, even in illuminating outline, what will be the invariant meanings (best) assigned to a particular group of problem terms, say, the group including 'knowledge' and 'justification'? The invariant meaning for a key expression, when worked out, will specify an ideal that we are prone to consider important, one for which we do not as yet have adequate expression. Presumably, this will be an ideal, as well, of which we have as yet only a very vague and dim idea. The better understanding of these "absolute ideals," though requiring detailed stipulational labor, would seem a deep enough achievement to satisfy certain philosophical inclinations.

We turn to the other side of the coin: As we learn more about the parameters of our temporary conversational concerns, as contextualist stipulational labors will encourage, we gain a better understanding of the texture of human communication. Contingencies that we take account of only implicitly may well be important to articulate, as would be done by one who specifies contextualist conventions for (contextualist descendants of our) 'know' and 'free'. These contingencies form an important part of the human situation, though they are not, of course, exhaustive. To have our situation better articulated will make us more aware of its particular character. To me, that also seems a worthwhile philosophical goal.

In the second place, there remains much to discuss, I think, about how one might try to create contexts, and get them accepted widely, in which extremely high standards are the ones in force. If this can be done systematically, which I doubt, then one might both accept a contextualist semantics for, say, 'know' and be a skeptic about knowledge. Now, as remarked in chapter III, the prospects for skepticism here look dim. But there may be rather subtle aspects of the situation as unobvious as they are powerful. On the other hand, if such contexts cannot be widely generated and maintained, as is my suspicion, it is philosophically interesting to say, in some detail, why that is so. As yet, this has not been done or, at least, not done very fully. Either way, then, there are matters here, both semantic and more worldly, that are open to fruitful philosophical inquiry.

In the third place, an area replete with relativity may yet have other aspects that are deeply problematic. The case of causation, I think, illustrates this well. Relativity concerns the manner in which a causal factor has the highest priority, whether absolutely or relative to certain conversational interests. But what is it that makes something, if anything ever does, even a *causal factor* in the occurrence of some particular happening? This matter has plenty of room for difficult philosophical analysis to take place, and it has been (almost) entirely untouched by our relativity considerations. Also, there seems plenty of room here for advocating skepticism about causal judgments and relations, for example, along lines suggested by Hume. A contextualist about 'cause', then, might think that there is no causation anyhow, thinking the appearance of any causal factors or relations to be only an illusion, both perceptual and intellectual.

The problem area of power and freedom provides another sort of illustration. As we discussed in chapter III, the problem of determinism's consequences is a conditional problem, not a categorical one. What, then, if the condition itself is not met, if determinism is not true but false? Then, at least some events will be undetermined even given all prior (and contemporaneous) considerations. Presumably, at least some of these undetermined events will be the performings of certain actions by certain human beings. So, for example, even with all of my intentions formed and my will discharged, it remains an open question whether my (right) arm moves at a certain time or not. If it does, as I intended it to, then perhaps I just get my wish; if not, then tough luck. Whether that arm then moves, it thus appears, is a random matter for failing to be a determined one. But, in such a case, it seems that *I* am not moving the arm at all; it is much like a spastic jerk. At least, it appears that I do not then move it of my own free will.

Considerations like these have led some philosophers to hold that human freedom actually requires determinism to be true and is impossible without it. Perhaps that is going too far. But there does seem to be a very vexing dilemma: Whether determinism is true or not, the idea of our autonomy, of our power and freedom to think and act, appears in jeopardy. Although the possibility of a contextualist semantics for the key terms may offer a little aid and comfort here, it does not seem to provide *nearly* enough to satisfy. There is plenty of room left still, it seems, both for some skepticism and for some deep philosophical analysis and reflection.

Philosophical relativity in a problem area does not mean that the problems in the area will yield easily to efforts at solution. For those whose first reaction is along headily optimistic lines, the illustrative case of causation, and that of freedom and power, should produce a more sober appreciation. Others, of course, will need no such sobering reminders. Indeed, many will react to relativity in quite the opposite way, with a severe pessimism right from the start: With such a great semantic mess abounding in a problem area, what hope is there for any clarity of pertinent thought, let alone any satisfactory philosophical solutions? Is such a gloomy reaction a warranted, realistic one?

From considerations of relativity, there is, I believe, no more reason for pessimism than for heady optimism. Indeed, there may be some slight reason for being less pessimistic than before when one reflects upon the paucity of progress throughout the history of philosophy. In areas infected with relativity, there is a mixture of matters; considerations generating the relativity are only some, not all, of those in the problem situation. Certain of the matters are indeterminate, thus inherently undecidable. But, if we can appreciate these aspects of the situation for what they are, then we might possibly separate them off or factor them out from the remaining matters or aspects. This may be very difficult to do, but it may not be impossible. If it is done, then we may confront rather directly those aspects of a given problem that may admit of some genuine solution to be arrived at nonarbitrarily. Without a relativistic aspect clouding what must be a difficult issue in any event, there will be one less reason for, or cause of, interminable disputation. There will be that much more of a chance for making philosophical progress.

The line of thinking just expressed offers nothing like a guarantee of any philosophical advance but only some cause to hope for that, perhaps a slight one. Even so, it is not bad to have some reason, however slight, to be hopeful. At any rate, preferring my relativistic reasonings to be taken in a hopeful spirit, I have tried to offer them in such a manner as might encourage an outlook that is more positive than pessimistic. Perhaps I have been deceiving myself in affecting such a positive presentation. Be that as it may, I do not see how I have deceived myself in arguing that our present situation is, in both language and thought, a widely relativistic one. So I continue to maintain the hypothesis, if not the belief, that this is so, no matter what prospects that may mean for the future of philosophy: good, bad, or neither.

Notes

Notes

Chapter I

1. But it may be that prospects of this sort are rather slight. Consider the problem of answering Zeno's challenge to (the belief in objective) motion. It often seems assumed that modern mathematics, or perhaps mathematical physics, provides an adequate answer. But, then, why do so many people keep thinking and writing variously on the problem, including so many that are sophisticated both scientifically and philosophically? Why is each writer so dissatisfied with the efforts of (almost all of) the others, feeling moved to make his own sophisticated efforts?

2. The most conspicuous instances of this are, I suppose, the second chapter of my book *Ignorance: A Case for Scepticism* (Oxford, 1975) and the chapter's ancestor, my paper "A Defense of Skepticism," *The Philosophical Review* LXXX (1971). There are many other instances.

3. As in "Logic and Conversation," Grice's (largely) unpublished William James Lectures. Some of this material is available, under the title of the whole, in *The Logic of Grammar*, edited by Donald Davidson and Gilbert Harman (Encino, Calif., and Belmont, Calif., 1975).

4. See David Lewis, *Convention* (Cambridge, Mass., 1969).

5. W. V. Quine, *Word and Object* (Cambridge, Mass., 1960).

6. Indeed, as is well known, Quine is most skeptical about whether the notion of definition even makes clear sense as applied to words of a natural language.

7. This is not to say, of course, that we could not develop a rich language with no such ambivalent expressions or aspects; I just doubt that we have done so. On the larger question, my position is entirely neutral.

8. Most especially, see Hilary Putnam, "The Refutation of Conventionalism," in *Semantics and Philosophy*, edited by Milton K. Munitz and Peter K. Unger (New York, 1974). (The paper is reprinted in Putnam's *Mind, Language and Reality* [Cambridge, 1975, 1979].)

It is perhaps worth noting that Quine's thesis *is logically compatible with* the indeterminacy that our own hypothesized relativity requires. But, then, why do I bother to criticize Quine's hypothesis? A good part of the reason is this: Although many have considered his thesis to be philosophically interesting, and rightly so, few have thought it to have any serious chance of being true or even of being anywhere close to the truth. So, I am moved to argue that our semantic relativity, and its required indeterminacy, have at least a *somewhat better chance at truth.*

9. See Max Black, "The Identity of Indiscernibles," in his *Problems of Analysis* (London, 1954).

10. See "The Refutation of Conventionalism."

11. "The Refutation of Conventionalism," pp. 241-42.

Chapter II

1. See my paper "A Defense of Skepticism," *The Philosophical Review* LXXX (1979), and my book *Ignorance: A Case for Scepticism* (Oxford, 1975).

2. David Lewis, "Scorekeeping in a Language Game," *Journal of Philosophical Logic* 8 (1979), pp. 353-54.

For a somewhat different (contextualist) treatment of absolute terms as a special sort of vague term, see Shane Andre, "Unger's Defense of Skepticism: New Wine in Old Bottles," *Canadian Journal of Philosophy* XII (1982), pp. 460-63. Given the discussion of Lewis soon to follow in the text, the accommodation of Andre's account within the framework of semantic relativity requires but a fairly straightforward variation.

3. Some have contended (in conversation) that the statement standardly made with the sentence 'Well, three people came to New York this morning' is the statement that *at least* three people came to New York this morning (rather than exactly three). I think that such a contention must rely on assigning an overly generous, improper semantics to 'three' or to 'three people'. But, for two reasons, this matter need not be pursued here. First, all of the points about getting the statement made suitably connected with an attended *relevant* thought will still hold good, even if, as is contended, the statement made is the generous one regarding the minimum. For, in such a case, though the statement will be a truth, it will be an obvious, fatuous one, not one informative about the parties in question. Second, all those points and all the points about truth-values can be made *uncontroversially* just by an obvious alteration of the uttered *sentence.* We simply consider, instead, the more explicit sentence 'Well, exactly three people came to New York this morning'. Or, for many contexts, we can consider 'Well, at most three people came to New York this morning'. In the body, then, I proceed directly with more germane issues.

4. On these matters, I am indebted to Allen Hazen.

5. Fred Dretske, "The Pragmatic Dimension of Knowledge," *Philosophical Studies* 40 (1981). In his slightly earlier book *Knowledge and the Flow of Information* (Cambridge, Mass., 1980), Dretske sketches the same position in a bit less detail or else sketches a very similar, less-detailed position.

6. Dretske, "The Pragmatic Dimension of Knowledge," pp. 364-66.

7. Dretske, "The Pragmatic Dimension of Knowledge," p. 378.

8. David Lewis, who (in conversation) introduced me to superinvariantism, makes the following interesting suggestion: Versions of superinvariantism in which we always are asserting a (single) *truth* are encouraged by many of the so-called "principles of charity." So much the worse, then, for all of those principles of charity. Better principles will be less concerned with tying our behavior (and thought) so directly to truth.

A principle of charity would have others agree (as much as possible) with ourselves, thus seeming to us to be *right* (about as much as possible). Any such principle will, of course, place some constraints on a semantics of our language. Now, among such charitable principles, some that are not outrageously bad will favor contextualism over (moderate) invariantism. That would discourage semantic relativity. But, as far as I can tell, no constraining principle anywhere in the neighborhood will be good enough to be adequate unless it is quite weak, weak enough so that it favors neither of our considered semantic approaches.

In a rather obvious way, all of this connects with what I said in section 2 of the present chapter.

9. See Nelson Goodman, *Fact, Fiction and Forecast* (London, 1954), Part III, "The New Riddle of Induction."

10. The question of accessibility will be treated at length in chapters IV and V.

Chapter III

1. Some philosophers dispute this: G. E. Moore seems to do so in various of his writings, and, much more recently, Peter Klein seems to do it in his *Certainty: A Refutation of Scepticism* (Minneapolis, Minn., 1981). Therefore, the point is at least minimally controversial. But such philosophers seem more motivated by the thought that they must deny skepticism than by sensitivity to the phenomena. Therefore, I suggest, the point is also at most minimally controversial.

2. In this connection, see the antiskeptical writing of David Lewis, "Scorekeeping in a Language Game," *Journal of Philosophical Logic* 8 (1979), and the skeptical writing of Jonathan Adler, "Skepticism and Universalizability," *The Journal of Philosophy* LXXVIII (1981).

3. The noted sentence contains the bracketed expressions 'at least fairly obviously'. Suppose, as is quite plausible, that, even on the invariantist account of 'know', a person need not know all of the logical consequences of anything he knows to be so. Then, the bracketed expression, or one with similar meaning, must apply. Suppose, as is only somewhat less plausible, such a stringent condition on 'know' is required by an adequate invariantist semantics for the term. In that case, no such expression need be used. Which is the right invariantist semantics; must we have such a modifying phrase or not? We need not decide the issue here; none of our main points depends upon its outcome.

4. Jonathan Adler, "Skepticism and Universalizability."

5. Some of the complexities are discussed in Fred Dretske, "The Pragmatic Dimension of Knowledge," *Philosophical Studies* 40 (1981). Further complexities are discussed in David Sanford, "Knowledge and Relevant Alternatives: Comments on Dretske," *Philosophical Studies* 40 (1981).

6. For a couple of recent examples, see B. L. Blose, "The 'Really' of Emphasis and the 'Really' of Restriction," *Philosophical Studies* 38 (1980), and Shane Andre, "Unger's Defense of Skepticism: New Wine in Old Bottles," *Canadian Journal of Philosophy* XII (1982).

7. Not for reasons of philosophical substance but for reasons of a personal and social character, I have chosen the area of knowledge: Because of my own interests, my previous writings have very often focused on this area. Because of that, certain of my readers would expect this focus in the present work as well; I have tried not to disappoint such expectations.

8. See David Lewis, "Scorekeeping in a Language Game," and an earlier paper by the same author, "The Paradoxes of Time Travel," *American Philosophical Quarterly* 13 (1976).

9. See my paper, "The Uniqueness in Causation," *American Philosophical Quarterly* 14 (1977).

10. Until recent years, I held to such a stringent characterization (in conversations with various philosophers). Carl Hempel, perhaps the most influential and stimulating thinker in

this area, has usually held to (at least) a *moderately* stringent position; thus, his idea that what we generally provide are not true explanations but "explanation sketches." See his *Aspects of Scientific Explanation* (New York, 1965). Perhaps the most lenient, most highly contextual position is that advocated by David Lewis in "Causal Explanation," *Philosophical Papers*, Volume II (New York and Oxford, forthcoming).

Chapter IV

1. See Benson Mates, "Synonymity," in Leonard Linsky (ed.), *Semantics and the Philosophy of Language* (Urbana, Ill., 1952), and especially Tyler Burge, "Belief and Synonymy," *The Journal of Philosophy* LXXV (1978).

2. This reply requires that we reject (unrestricted application of) a *principle of compositionality of meaning*, according to which the meaning of a whole sentence is a (straightforward) function of the meaning(s) of its parts. Consider the phrase 'the belief that the table is flat is the same belief as the belief that the table is'. When we conjoin this with the word 'flat', we get an obvious truth. When we conjoin it with the apparently (or arguably) synonymous expression 'such that nothing could be flatter', our reply runs, we do not get a truth. So, on this reply, the resulting sentences are not synonymous. Consequently, on this reply, the considered principle must be doubted or restricted. But, then, perhaps this is not actually a fully general, acceptable principle.

3. For a particularly interesting treatment of this, see Howard Darmstadter, "Consistency of Belief," *The Journal of Philosophy* LXVIII (1971).

Chapter V

1. Hilary Putnam, "It Ain't Necessarily So," *The Journal of Philosophy* LIX (1962).

2. Though most philosophers ignore the fact, it must be acknowledged that different contexts can induce, or encourage, different dominant responses. I discuss this complex matter, important for certain questions, in my recent paper, "Toward a Psychology of Common Sense," *American Philosophical Quarterly* 19 (1982). For the questions that are presently before us, however, this variable contextual factor matters very little if at all. Therefore, I will tend to ignore it in the present work.

3. In his early paper, "It Ain't Necessarily So," Putnam seems very much in conflict; he exhibits, I believe, considerable sensitivity. But in his later paper, "The Meaning of 'Meaning'," Putnam can see no conflict to be present, or so it appears. See, especially, pp. 243-44 of "The Meaning of 'Meaning' " as it appears in Putnam's *Mind, Language and Reality* (Cambridge, 1975, 1979). (My references are to the first paperback edition, 1979.) At the present time, then, the existence of genuine dominated responses cannot be overemphasized.

4. Saul Kripke's main work on the subject is his "Naming and Necessity," first published in *Semantics of Natural Language*, edited by D. Davidson and G. Harman (Dordecht, 1972), and now available as a book, *Naming and Necessity* (Cambridge, Mass., 1980). My references will be to the book.

Hilary Putnam's main contribution to the theory is "The Meaning of 'Meaning'," first published in *Language, Mind and Knowledge*, edited by K. Gunderson (Minneapolis, Minn., 1975). The paper, along with other writings by Putnam on the subject, is reprinted in his *Mind, Language and Reality*.

The other most prominent contributor to this theory is Keith Donnellan, as in his "Proper Names and Identifying Descriptions," *Synthese* 21 (1970), and in his "Speaking of Nothing," *The Philosophical Review* LXXXIII (1974). Since Donnellan's work is mainly concerned with proper names, whereas I am concerned mainly with common words, I will not refer to his writings in what follows.

5. Kripke, *Naming and Necessity*, pp. 135-36.

6. To say that the causal theory for proper names is plausible is not, of course, to say that it is free of difficulties or that it is correct or even that it is nearly correct, issues on which I wish to remain neutral. For some interesting criticisms of this theory on proper names, see Paul Ziff, "About Proper Names," *Mind* 86 (1977). Quite a few other philosophers also have presented difficulties for the theory. But my impression of the criticisms leveled so far is that they point to restrictions on this theory of names or to modifications required in the theory rather than to some fundamental error in the view; this, whether or not the view does have fundamental errors.

7. In "The Meaning of 'Meaning'," Putnam sometimes advocates such a more "current" version of the theory. (At other times in the paper, however, he endorses Kripke's historical version, which is incompatible with the current version. In "Putnam's Theory on the Reference of Substance Terms," *The Journal of Philosophy* LXXIII [1976], Eddy Zemach notes this ambivalence.)

8. Even as at least *some* version of the causal theory is initially rather *plausible* as regards *proper names*, so *any* version, it seems, is initially rather *implausible* as regards common *words*. Apart from its ability to treat examples, *on the whole*, this theory of words does not appear a very appealing one. Now, this is not to say that, before such treatment, nothing at all can be said on behalf of the causal theory. Rather, the point is one of overall balance: Initially, whatever seems in favor of this theory for words is more than offset by what seems to go against it.

9. In "The Meaning of 'Meaning'," Putnam discusses examples (some from Rogers Albritton) that make it seem that the causal theory should apply to such words as 'pencil' and 'pediatrician'. In "Toward a Psychology of Common Sense," I discuss an example that makes it seem that the theory applies even to 'bachelor' (if it really applies to any common nouns at all).

10. In this more generous vein, we may recognize as well a third sort of response as a typical one to our example: that only the past robots will have been cats, not the future feline animals. This is the only response that, on the accepted method, is favorable for the causal theory. Who makes it? As far as I can tell, it is made mainly by those who know of the causal theory. If that is so, then perhaps little can be learned from this sort of response here. But even that is not to say that this response is wrong while one of the others is somehow the correct philosophical response. Rather, the relation of philosophical theories to examples, and to responses, is far more complex than such assessments allow.

11. The contrasting pair of cases just sketchily presented is more radical than those Kripke explicitly considers. Where I talk of robots versus animals in relation to the topic of cats, Kripke talks of reptiles versus mammals. But, especially from the viewpoint of the causal theory, the main points will be the same, regardless of the degree of the imagined departure.

12. Accordingly, a little, but then only a very little, will be achieved by adverting to this more current sort of causal view. This remark presupposes, of course, that such a more current view does no better than did the historical version in respect of the examples already discussed in previous sections. But that supposition is correct, as the reader can easily verify.

13. We must allow, of course, that a common word can sometimes change its meaning, just as we must allow that a proper name can change its denotation. In general, when a word changes its meaning, there will occur a correlative shift in its reference as well. On these matters, see Gareth Evans, "The Causal Theory of Names," *Aristotelian Society Supplementary Volume* XLVII (1973), pp. 195-96. Also see Kripke, *Naming and Necessity*, p. 163.

14. In his recent book, *Designation* (New York, 1981), Michael Devitt attempts to outline a sort of causal theory that deals with examples like those introduced by Evans, "The Causal Theory of Names," and others. See especially chapter 7, section 2. With regard to (most of) the examples considered here, Devitt's suggestions are, I believe less than convincing; perhaps they are even irrelevant. Compare them with the psychological approach to intuitions that I will employ in the next section.

15. In "The Causal Theory of Reference," *Philosophical Studies* 43 (1983), I present and discuss a number of these troublesome examples. Also relevant is some of my discussion in "Toward a Psychology of Common Sense."

16. For a more detailed treatment of these matters, see my "Toward a Psychology of Common Sense."

17. For related examples, we focus on related beliefs of differing strengths. Suppose that, in the case of past robots and future animals, the animals to be placed on earth were not created suddenly but were for a long time on Mars. Then, if those distant animals are cats, as we take it, there will have been plenty of cats in the past anyway; we do not need past robots as cats to make true our past-directed existence belief. Still, we respond so that the past robots are cats. Why is that? We do need the past robots to make true this related belief: that, in much of the past, many people on earth have encountered many cats. That belief, too, is a very powerful past-directed attitude, and we respond so that it will seem true to us. In contrast, the correlative future-directed belief is not so powerful: that, in much of the future, many people on earth will encounter many cats. So, to an example in which feline animals live only on Mars in the future and feline robots are on earth, we do *not* respond by taking the robots to be cats. Although there is a bit more complexity here, the basic structure of explanation is the same.

18. In "The Meaning of 'Meaning'," Putnam begins his presentation of Twin Earth cases on p. 223. His discussion of the import of these cases, both positive and negative, runs throughout the paper.

19. See my "The Causal Theory of Reference," especially its section 7, "Twin Earth Revisited."

20. In conversation, and also in correspondence, David Lewis has adduced a number of considerations that take some of the sting out of the noted bias. Although his points are at least somewhat effective, they do not, in my judgment, fully dispel the air of irrationality.

Chapter VI

1. Indeed, this problem carries over to many verbs of action and so to many alleged actions, and perhaps to all. See my papers "The Uniqueness in Causation," *American Philosophical Quarterly* 14 (1977), and "Impotence and Causal Determinism," *Philosophical Studies* 31 (1977).

2. A detailed version of this argument is given in my book *Ignorance* (Oxford, 1975), pp. 199-214. Further supporting linguistic evidence is there provided on pp. 214-26. A closely related argument is offered in my paper "Skepticism and Nihilism," *Nous* 14 (1980), mainly on pp. 531-34.

3. See *Ignorance*, pp. 231-42.

4. See W. V. Quine, "Two Dogmas of Empiricism," in his *From a Logical Point of View* (Cambridge, Mass., 1953).

5. See H. P. Grice and P. F. Strawson, "In Defense of a Dogma," *The Philosophical Review* LXV (1956).

6. See Grice and Strawson, "In Defense of a Dogma."

7. Various philosophers, perhaps most notably Donald Davidson, have argued that this

represents no genuine possibility. Although I am not wholly unimpressed by these arguments, I am not convinced by them either. Therefore, I will pursue the matter, at least briefly. See Davidson's "On the Very Idea of a Conceptual Scheme," *Proceedings and Addresses of the American Philosophical Association* XLVII (1974).

8. Actually, in the system of the ancient Greek philosopher Anaximander, there appears a problem of dryness. But this problem has nothing at all to do with semantics, on the one hand, and, on the other, is not of any general philosophical interest or importance.

Index

Index

131

132 / Index

Peter Unger was educated at Swarthmore College and at St. John's College, Oxford, where he earned his D. Phil. in 1966. He taught for several years at the University of Wisconsin, and is now professor of philosophy at New York University. Unger is the author of *Ignorance: A Case for Scepticism.*